TITANS OF BASS

The Tactics, Habits, and Routines from over 130 of the World's Best

KJ JENSEN

Backbeat Books

Essex, Connecticut

An imprint of Globe Pequot, the trade division of
The Rowman & Littlefield Publishing Group, Inc.
4501 Forbes Blvd., Ste. 200
Lanham, MD 20706
www.rowman.com

Distributed by NATIONAL BOOK NETWORK

British Library Cataloguing in Publication Information available

Library of Congress Cataloging-in-Publication Data

Names: Jensen, KJ, author.
Title: Titans of bass : the tactics, habits, and routines from over 130 of
  the world's best / KJ Jensen.
Description: Guilford, Connecticut : Backbeat Books, 2022. | Includes
  index.
Identifiers: LCCN 2021059267 (print) | LCCN 2021059268 (ebook) | ISBN
  9781493062874 (paperback) | ISBN 9781493062881 (epub)
Subjects: LCSH: Bass guitar—Instruction and study. | Bass guitarists.
Classification: LCC MT599.B4 J48 2022 (print) | LCC MT599.B4 (ebook) |
  DDC 787.87/193—dc23
LC record available at https://lccn.loc.gov/2021059267
LC ebook record available at https://lccn.loc.gov/2021059268

♾™ The paper used in this publication meets the minimum requirements of American
National Standard for Information Sciences—Permanence of Paper for Printed Library
Materials, ANSI/NISO Z39.48-1992

TITANS OF BASS

Contents

Foreword

The passion to play the bass, or to spend your life playing any particular instrument . . . where does it come from? Maybe nobody knows the answer to that, but this book will walk you down the road, from step one, to being a bassist. Its advice is unique and built upon experience, but each chapter is informed and enlightened by statements by bassists themselves—an amazing assembly of experienced, successful bassists who have taken that walk themselves and have a lot to offer those who are considering setting out on it. As a bassist of many years myself, I am thrilled at basking in the advice, articulations, and admonitions of these players—Titans, indeed, of the bass.

—Tony Levin

Tony Levin has played bass in the classical, jazz, and rock fields, notably with Peter Gabriel, King Crimson, John Lennon, and Pink Floyd.

How to Use This Book

Thank you for buying this guide! Because I value each and every one of you, there are some free gifts to take part in! Before you do anything, please do these three things:

1. Log on to http://www.bassguitarbeginner.com/ and register and sign up for the challenge.
2. Join the "Titans of Bass" Facebook group at https://www.facebook.com/groups/2548463212118457.
3. Visit "Titans of Bass" YouTube channel at https://www.youtube.com/channel/UCPTsxR-dP0_zGgKVaJ6SFpg.

Go to Welcome video: Countdown Day 0. Please subscribe and Like. Please follow along on the website, YouTube channel, and Facebook group and perform the daily tasks. You then will be on your way to perhaps becoming a future "Titan of Bass"!

Preface
by the Author

How Bass Saved My Life

There I sat in the middle of the doctor's office, slumped over, almost in tears. The doctor spoke softly, trying to be supportive. I was a wreck, a massive ball of emotions.

It was always rough in the wintertime for me, but this winter was too much. I was down in the dumps, in debt from a failed business venture, and smack dab in a premature midlife crisis in my mid-thirties. I had finally had enough of being depressed that I decided to get some help. I figured that admitting it is the first step to doing something about it.

After a few basic questions, he determined that I would need some help with my problems. He then asked a question that helped save my life. "Is there anything that you can do that still makes you happy?" he asked quizzically in his eastern European accent.

I had to think about that. I sat on the examination table thoroughly exhausted, dejected, and depressed. The vivid image of my 2008 Roseburst Ernie Ball Music Man Sterling popped up in my mind. It was a joy to play, and playing it made me happy each and every time I did so.

"I still . . . like . . . playing bass," I stammered, the words sticking in my throat.

"Ok, then I will give you an assignment that you have to follow every day," he replied. "You should play bass for one hour a day at minimum. You need to get back on your feet, your family depends on you," he expressed, putting a supportive hand on my arm.

"Ok," I replied. That's the moment my life changed. Playing the bass wasn't just an interesting pastime at that point, it was necessary for my survival and well-being. It now had the potential of saving my life.

So I kept at it, with all the passion and dedication of someone who was given an ultimatum, albeit an enjoyable one. I played bass every day. I watched a million YouTube videos on the bass greats. I played until my fingers and ears hurt. I eventually got better—not just at playing bass but at feeling happier. My depression subsided each and every day the more that I kept playing. Within a few months, playing my bass helped me crawl out of my depressive state, which ultimately saved my life. The bass saved my life!

That's When I Had a Million-Dollar Idea!

What if others could be helped with the power of the bass like I was? What if my story could resonate with young people and give them something worthwhile to pursue? Could the bass also "save" their lives? Could playing it keep them out of trouble, away from harmful drugs and bad influences that sadly exist in our world today?

I had to do something about this magical, musical, and amazing instrument that deserves more attention than it gets! My desire to learn bass helped me crawl out of my depressive state, and I thought I could help others by sharing my story.

What if I had the power to share my story with the world? Then I thought, what would be the best way to amplify my message so the most people could hear it? I thought about that for a while. How could I inspire others to "give bass a chance"?

I thought back to all my bass heroes who inspired me to pick up the instrument. What if I could use their knowledge and experience to add rocket fuel to this potential project? What if I could, as the great Tony Robbins always said, "model the masters" and use their wisdom to kickstart this story?

Then it all clicked. I had a massive brain fart!

Preface
by Robbie Shakespeare

After hearing KJ's story of how the "bass saved his life," I can totally relate. It truly sum-marizes my relationship with music in general, and the bass in particular. I grew up in the Dunkirk ghetto in Kingston, Jamaica. Life was rough and to survive, you had to kill or be killed.

I grew up as a "Rudie" and was constantly chased by the police. Back then I could run! I had to survive "by any means necessary" with all the other kids my age. Many of us got killed by other gangsters or the police. My life expectancy as a Rudie was only a few decades at best.

Then one day, God grabbed me and took me to Randy's studio. Aston "Family Man" Barrett was there, laying down tracks for Bob Marley. I walked straight up to him: "I want you to teach me bass." He knew my bad-boy reputation. He replied, "Alright, at least that's better than the trouble you are getting into."

The same day, I found a way to get my hands on a bass. Barrett showed me one chord and told me to practice it until the next day. For several months, he came to check on me every day. I worked so hard at playing it that the tips of my fingers bled. I had to cut up bands of fabric to wrap around my fingers to be able to keep practicing. To this day, my fingertips still feel soft.

Then one day, Barrett introduced me to Bunny Lee as his protégé. Six months later, I was playing on two songs from Bob Marley's album, Catch A Fire. I give thanks every day that God showed me another way out. My mentor Barrett acted as God's helper on Earth and kept me out of trouble and death. It's true, the bass really saved my life!

—Robbie Shakespeare

Robbie Shakespeare—reggae artist extraordinaire, world's most prolific bassist, and in-demand producer alongside his longtime collaborator Sly Dunbar—admits he was "humbled" upon learning he made *Rolling Stone*'s recent list of the "50 Greatest Bassists of All Time."

Acknowledgments

Thanks to you, the reader. Perhaps you are interested in music and want to give the bass a chance. Thanks for taking your valuable time to go on this challenge with me.

And what a journey it's been so far. I remember the hours of interviews, the amazing and funny stories, and all the new perspectives on music that I learned. It was great fun and I enjoyed conversing and meeting so many amazing musicians and amazing people!

So many to thank! Thanks to John Cerullo at Backbeat Books for believing in and taking on this project and for answering my many questions that kept me on the path to completion. Thanks to his assistant Barbara for getting stuff done on the administrative side.

Thanks to my wife and brother-in-law for having the patience to let me take on and finish this mammoth project.

A special thanks to all the Titans of Bass! Without their life experiences and dedication to the pursuit of the low end, this book would never have been born. Of course, a big thank you to all their assistants and management who were ready and willing to help with interview setups, requests, and a lot of small details that make up a huge project like this.

I'd like to thank each and every Titan of Bass for their patience, their time, their expertise, and their amazing stories. Many of them shared details of their lives and stories that have never publicly been published. I feel honored that I got the chance to report and document them.

I would like to thank each of them individually, but I fear that I might not have the room due to the multitude interviewed. Please know that I appreciate each and every story and account that I went through.

Thanks for caring!

—KJ Jensen

Day 1

The Titans of Bass Project Was Born!

Bass is the place.

—Barry Adamson

When I was a young pup, I was a very shy, introverted kid. Being in my own world most of the time, things changed when I hit first grade. You see that's when I learned how to read. To me it was the most magical thing ever. When I learned, I couldn't stop; I read and read and read. I entered reading contests and won. I entered one contest over two hundred times, meaning I read over two hundred books! My love of reading and learning transformed into a love of writing many years later.

Since I was a reporter, writer, and entrepreneur for close to two decades, I knew how to interview people and write original articles. My "brain fart" was this: I would reach out to all my bass heroes and ask them how and why they got started on the bass. I would ask what best practices they used to get better, and why they loved the bass as much as I did.

So I got to work. I made a list of my bass heroes. But I don't know everything, sometimes I think I don't know anything. So it was research to the rescue!

I needed to find the cream of the crop, the best of the best, the "Titans of Bass." I tackled this in several steps. After every step I would catalogue the names of the bass players that I had unearthed.

I made a list:

1. I google-searched to find the best living bassists, those who are on all the "top 100 bassists" lists, those who have all the technical prowess and long careers—the best practitioners.

2. I looked up the top fifty best-selling artists of all time. I then checked out these acts to find those sessions and live musicians who played on these albums. This led me to google "best session bass players" and so forth.

3. Then, I looked at all my favorite records, songs, bands, and so forth, and picked the bassists that weren't on the above lists. Some of these players were also super influential—a lot of choices in the punk, metal, and alternative fields.

Whew! I knew I had the "holy grail" as it were of players who had played on the best-selling and most influential songs of all time. I had a ton of potential bassists to interview, literally hundreds! This was getting exciting! It included bass wizards from a ton of genres: rock, pop, hip-hop, rap, country, punk, metal, hard rock, folk, dance, alternative, funk, boogie, blues, the list goes on.

I wanted this project to have a global perspective. So I went and accumulated a "Dream 100 List." These one hundred interviews would give me an amazing wealth of knowledge to boil down. What would the similarities and differences of these bassists be?

So I went to work and rolled up my sleeves. I asked all my interviewees the best ways to help absolute beginners pick up the instrument and find out if bass is for them.

By the end of several months I had a list of over 130 successful interviews! Success! So, according to the list, the active participants in this project contributed to thirty-three of the top fifty best-selling artists of all time! We are talking about over two billion units sold—that's billion with a "B"!

I tallied the actual list of the bands, groups, and artists that these 131 bass titans were involved with. The number was mind boggling—over 1,000 of the top known acts of all time!

After many interviews, I began to view myself as the ultimate experimenter. I started to test out the practices and theories in my own playing. I figured if I can't make the guidance work in my busy and messy life, then I shouldn't be showing others how to do it. I became the "Bass Guinea Pig." Wow, that sounds like a cool band or album name! What I learned helped me advance more quickly in my playing, saving me countless hours of wasted effort and frustration.

My main goal of this project was to use all the wisdom from the "Titans of Bass" to create the future "Titans of Bass." I think that would be so amazing! This "challenge" is the quickest way possible to immerse yourself and see if the bass is something you want to continue playing.

I boiled the "cream" of the interviews down into small chunks and arranged them in sequential steps in the form of a 14-day challenge. The challenge is to get an absolute beginner to pick up the bass and learn how to play and perform a simple song. In this way you can determine if the bass is for you and if your bass journey will continue.

This is not a coffee-table book that sits on your shelf but an actionable guide. I want you to discover, "Is the bass for me? Can the bass save my life?"

Two Principles to Live By

While interviewing, I was especially inspired by these three quotations:

1. "I have lived by two adages for my whole life. The first is 'Less is more,' The second is 'KISS: Keep It Simple, Stupid.'" —Russell Jackson
2. "One adage that I try to live by is: 'Any idiot can design something complicated. It takes a genius to simplify.'" —Phil Soussan
3. "Make the bass your life. Just listen." —Verdine White

I took these amazing bits of advice and made sure that I, like a great bass player, gave each and every day and activity the right amount of heft, instruction, fun, work, and balance that it needed to help make sure that you have been given every chance to give the bass a good honest try. I let the Titans speak for themselves. I always try to keep it simple to make sure your bass journey is fun, entertaining, and educational.

Don't get me wrong. This journey is not to make you a virtuoso like Victor Wooten overnight. I want to see if the bass is for you. I don't want you to buy thousands of dollars of gear that collects dust and never gets played.

I want you to also make this challenge a mission as well. For the next fourteen days, if you follow along and complete the daily activities, you should be able to play a simple song live in front of your friends.

If you are serious about learning the bass, love challenges, are teachable and patient, love music, and want to learn directly from the best bassists of all time, then please accept this "Titan of Bass" mission statement.

Please read aloud:

My mission, if I choose to accept it, will be to follow each of the daily action steps over the next fourteen days. This will result in me playing a live performance of the Titans of Bass song for my friends and family. When I complete this mission, I will be a future "Titan of Bass"!

Who Are the Titans of Bass?

So, I know you must be curious, who are these Titans? I will now give you a quick list of them. Rather than give you all 131 bios of them in this chapter, I will give you a bunch per day. This will give you an incentive and encouragement to keep at it through your 14-day journey. I'm proud to announce the "Titans of BASS"!

Victor Wooten	Leland Sklar
Billy Sheehan	Mike Watt
Justin Chancellor	Sean Lennon
John Patitucci	Bakithi Kumalo
Geezer Butler	Christian McBride
Jeff Berlin	Kai Eckhardt
Ron Carter	Michael Manring
Stuart Hamm	Hadrien Feraud
Jack Casady	Bill Laswell
George Porter Jr.	Percy Jones
Verdine White	Neil Jason
Abraham Laboriel	Leo Lyons
Nathan East	Gail Ann Dorsey

Horace Panter

Suzi Quatro

Dave Pegg

Billy Gould

Kasim Sulton

Stu Cook

Dave Larue

Brad Smith

Trey Gunn

Bruce Thomas

Ariane Cap

Guy Pratt

Jah Wobble

Darryl Jones

Mark Stoermer

dUg Pinnick

Kenny Lee Lewis

Eva Gardner

Liam Wilson

Bjorn Englen

Colin Edwin

Kenny Passarelli

Scott Thunes

Derek Frank

Jon Button

Julie Slick

Roy Vogt

Barry Adamson

Tonina Saputo

Dennis Dunaway

Joe Bouchard

Klaus Flouride

Chuck Dukowski

Glen Matlock

Gerald Casale

Ben Ellis

Arthur Barrow

Oneida James

Daniel Miranda

Wyzard

Tony Green

Jim Pons

Mark Bedford

Rudy Sarzo

Michael Lepond

Basil Fearrington

Bryan Beller

Damian Erskine

Phil Soussan

Stephen Jay

Steve Fossen

James LoMenzo

Starr Cullars

Scott Ambush

Wayne Jones

Ronnie "Dawg" Robson

Rev Jones

Scott Brown

Harley Flanagan

Bunny Brunel

Kyle Eastwood

Monique Ortiz

Michael Dempsey

Miki Santamaria

Mark Burgess

Clinton J. Conley

Marc van Wageningen

Joshua Cohen

Davey Faragher

Jasper Høiby

Hansford Rowe

Angeline Saris

James Cook

Jean Millington

Kern Brantley

Kevin Keith

Rob Stoner

Adam Nitti

Jason Raso

Chris Dale

Gina Schwarz

Anais Noir

Rob Ruiz

Federico Malaman

Mick Harvey

Gary Lachman

Armand Sabal-Lecco

Shem Schroeck

Bubby Lewis

Blaise Sison

Liran Donin

Joan Armatrading

Manou Gallo

Kinley Wolfe

Peter Trewavas

Tom Griesgraber

Shaun Munday

Henrik Linder

Davey Rimmer

Shorty B

Larry Lee

Peter Griffin

Russell Jackson

JD Pinkus

Mary Huff

Who Have the "Titans of Bass" Played With?

The Titans of Bass have played with, were members of, recorded, produced, or played in stages with the following top acts of all time:

The Beatles, Michael Jackson, David Bowie, The Eagles, Billy Joel, Led Zeppelin, Elton John, Pink Floyd, AC/DC, George Strait, The Rolling Stones, Barbra Streisand, Madonna, Bruce Springsteen, Whitney Houston, Van Halen, U2, Celine Dion, Neil Diamond, Journey, Kenny G, Shania Twain, Kenny Rogers, Guns N' Roses, Santana, Reba McEntire, Eric Clapton,

Simon & Garfunkel, Rod Stewart, Foreigner, 2PAC, Bob Dylan, Queen, Phil Collins, Black Sabbath, Kiss, Tool, Hot Tuna, Jefferson Airplane, Earth Wind & Fire, CCR, Iggy Pop, Blondie, Tower of Power, Ozzy Osbourne, Quiet Riot, Steve Miller, Faith No More, BB King, Iron Maiden, Heart, Dixie Dregs, Mother's Finest, Ten Years After, Pink, Black Flag, Dead Kennedys, Alice Cooper, The Killers, The Smashing Pumpkins, The Who, Peter Gabriel, Meatloaf, Shakira, Blue Öyster Cult, Lou Reed, Sheryl Crow, Joe Cocker, Stevie Wonder, TOTO, Kenny Loggins, Daft Punk, The Bee Gees, Quincy Jones, Lenny Kravitz, Devo, The National, Sting, Barry White, Dolly Parton, Aretha Franklin, Carole King, Michael Bolton, The Guess Who, Toni Braxton, Bette Midler, Randy Newman, Cher, The Mars Volta, Roxy Music, Hall & Oates, Cyndi Lauper, Dire Straits, Ted Nugent, Butthole Surfers, Joe Satriani, Steve Vai, Minutemen, The Stooges, Frank Zappa, The Mothers of Invention, Nick Cave, Elvis Costello, Funkadelic, George Clinton, Jethro Tull, Sly and the Family Stone, and so many more!!!

Wow! What a list!

Let's Ask the Titans: Why Play the Bass?

The whole function of the bass is to make other people sound better. It's also one of the easiest instruments to learn to play well enough to play with other people quickly. It's not like piano or guitar with many chords or drums where you have four limbs to coordinate. With the bass you just push a note down and it sounds good, and you play one note at a time. It's also a very powerful instrument. A lot of the control of the music comes from the instrument. You get to learn both sides of life with the bass—both the subtle and powerful side.

—Victor Wooten

There is always a demand to fill the noble and vital role of holding it all together as part of the low end club.

—Justin Chancellor

How many people really get to do what they absolutely love in life? Very few. A lot of people whine about their jobs and have countdown clocks on how many days until retirement. I pinch myself every day on how lucky I am to be making music. I still look forward to every day as much as the first day I started playing over fifty years ago.

—LEE SKLAR

I think the bass player is the cool one in the group. You don't want to look like you're working too hard back there, but you are driving the car. So you gotta relax.

—GAIL ANN DORSEY

Playing bass gives you a foundation in rhythm and harmony at the same time. I think it's a little easier to get started for a beginner than a guitar is. It's the foundation of the rhythm section.

—NATHAN EAST

Learning the bass is less intimidating than other instruments. Playing important notes that "anchor" the music with a larger fret ratio is also easier than learning flashy guitar leads or complicated keyboard melodies that could "sink" a performance. You can just lay back and "steer the ship."

—MARY HUFF

I chose the bass because, at the time, rhythm guitar wasn't required in the type of music that I followed like Cream, Jimi Hendrix, and Led Zeppelin.

—GEEZER BUTLER

You should play bass if you have the feeling for it. I never went from guitar to bass, which happens a lot.

—SUZI QUATRO

You should choose the bass because you simply enjoy more of the social aspects of playing music. Bass is the conductor, the conduit, and the catalyst.

—SHAUN MUNDAY

The bass is the "interesting" part of the rhythm section. It can play with the drums or against the drums. It has both melodic and harmonic content, so it's able to work with the vocals and other parts of the arrangement, as well. It's not limited to being a timekeeper.

—STU COOK

You have to go with your heart and your feelings. If you pick up a sax and your heart feels good, go with it. I played trumpet and piano for many years, but when I picked up the bass, everything else disappeared. That was a sign. I fell in love with the bass and it wasn't practice anymore. I would just walk around with it attached to my body and still haven't stopped.

—Neil Jason

There are not as many bass players out there so there are a lot of opportunities to play. The bass also suits my personality. I'm mellow, not super extroverted or talkative. I love sitting in the background and holding down a mellow groove. Let the others be the crazy rock star in the front. The bass is like the pie crust—you don't notice it's not there until all you have is a bunch of fruit on the table.

—Jon Button

Learning bass is a personal commitment. It is something that will take time and effort. I agreed to follow my inner voice that told me each time I played rhythmic bass I was at peace with me.

—Manou Gallo

It's a great instrument that encompasses both harmony and rhythm. It traditionally only has four strings, so you are limited as to how many notes you can play at one time.

—Scott Ambush

It isn't for the fans and adoration, as the guitar players and lead singers get that. It is an instrument that is fun to play and has lots of room for exploration. Plus every good band needs and should have a great bass player.

—George Porter Jr.

Don't play the bass unless it calls you. It's in your soul more than the guitar is. Ultimately, it's an expression that's at the center of your core more than at your fingertips. You are the backbone of the band.

—Brad Smith

The bass can be applied to any genre. If a kid is interested in several genres of music, I would recommend bass. Guitars aren't in every genre. There is so much to do with bass.

It never gets boring. I had super bad ADD when I was younger. I wanted to play every-thing. I was floored at what I could with a bass.

—Tonina Saputo

If you want to be the coolest kid on the block, open the window and start thumping. I remember there was a band called Renegade Soundwave with a record called "Women Respond To Bass." What a great title!

—Barry Adamson

You will get more gigs playing bass. There are just less people playing bass over guitar and drums. Supply and demand. It's also the most powerful instrument.

—Bryan Beller

Bass is a passive-aggressive instrument—you secretly control the whole band.

—Davey Faragher

One reason that I got involved in so many projects is because you can get in there as a bassist. For every brick building, there is mortar. We are like the mortar guys! The bass is kind of like glue. What's glue without something to stick to? Just a puddle. And I don't want a bunch of puddles out there!

—Mike Watt

It's often overlooked and underappreciated. When you are a good, solid bass player, and do the job properly, people call you. There are so many brilliant guitar players and singers, but to find a good bass player is special. It's a really cool special instrument that offers so much to a band when done right. The bass is a special instrument. It's a special niche with a very supportive community. It's made up of a great group of people who love what they do each and every day.

—Eva Gardner

Every band needs a bass player.

—Blaise Sison

Bass is one of the greatest instruments ever. It changed rock and roll and R&B forever. The best bass players are actually students of music.

—Verdine White

Bass and drums are the most important parts of rock and roll. If you have a band with a great bass player and drummer, it's going to be a great band, even if the guitarist and vocalist are just ok. But if you have a band with a really great guitar player and really great singer but the bass and drums suck, you are not going to want to listen to it. You just can't.

—SEAN LENNON

My bass instructor in college always told me: "A bass player will always eat." There were always too many singers and guitarists but not enough bass players. When I went to the original School of Rock in Philadelphia, we had to perform live shows. There were so many guitar players but only two bass players. I got to play half the shows! When I pick up the bass, it's like meditation. It's sort of an unconscious thing. Music is my therapy.

—JULIE SLICK

Bass is fun in an aspect that you can play some songs by just hammering eight notes on one note. So you will probably learn to play some songs that you like without too many problems.

—HENRIK LINDER

The bass offers so many chances to enjoy and play a wide variety of music and the opportunity to join in with other musicians no matter the level of playing you have achieved.

—DAVE PEGG

Bass is beautiful. When I'm playing bass I feel like I'm "driving" the band. I think music is built like a pyramid. The bass is on the bottom layer and the singer or the lead instrument is on the top with the other stuff in between. They won't be shit without bass supporting them from the bottom. In the structure of music, the bass is super important. A couple of years ago they did scientific tests on the components of music and how people listen. They would repeatedly play the same song to people, each time removing an instrument. The one that made the most difference to the listener was the removal of the bass.

—ARTHUR BARROW

I played on six live BB King albums. My job was to make the band sound good all the time. If you want to make a living at playing the bass, become a rhythm player and keep the band going. That's your job.

—RUSSELL JACKSON

The best bands have the best bass players. You get an incredible amount of freedom along with a tremendous responsibility. To be successful you have to be willing to accept both those aspects of it. You have the capability of controlling and manipulating rhythm, harmony, and melody. When you listen to great bass playing you are really listening to little stories. They may not draw immediate focus because there are so many other beautiful parts going on. You can discover all these little melodies and rhythmic things going on, all the notes that aren't immediately apparent to your ears.

—DANIEL MIRANDA

It's a calling. If it happens to be the bass that calls you, you might appreciate how easy it is to get started, how much fun it is to play, and how far you can go with it.

—STEPHEN JAY

For some reason, the low end of the bass creates a very comforting feeling to me. It's like laying on a waterbed. It makes me feel safe. It comforts and calms me down. It's like being in my mother's womb. When I play the bass it's like a voice. You have to feel deep feelings to make great music.

—dUg PINNICK

Anybody can play the bass, there's no secret to it. It's a matter of how much time you spend and information that you want to learn. There are always opportunities, you just have to go for it.

—BAKITHI KUMALO

To be successful, you have to love the way that bass resonates. Bass doesn't have to be relegated to background music. It holds the whole thing together.

—KLAUS FLOURIDE

When I was in the studio with Bad Seeds in 1986, some people were saying that I "was wasted on the bass." I couldn't agree. In no way, shape, or form was it wasted on me. Bass is so critical to the feel of everything. It really is a fundamental instrument. Yet it's underappreciated in some ways. A lot of listeners don't realize what it is doing and don't really hear it.

—MICK HARVEY

The beauty of the bass is that it takes a minute to learn and a lifetime to master.

—CHRIS DALE

The bass is essential. When a lot of guitar players are out of work, bass players still get work. It seems like bands always need bassists for some reason. It's not as glamorous as being a lead guitar player or singer. But, depending on your personality, the bass is a really great place to be.

For certain people, the bass is their calling. This is fantastic! Every kid should try out the bass along with all the other instruments like the guitar, ukulele, and piano. It's simpler than other instruments as it's played one note at a time. The trick is how to play those notes with groove and feel. It is really a massage for the mind and helps to move other things forward by laying down the emotional foundation of the song. The bass can sit in the back and relax. It can also make or break the band. When I pick up the bass, it's like an old friend. It makes me feel great.

—JOE BOUCHARD

Steve Vai once told me "I'm not that great of a guitar player." He told me that he has to slow down a tune until he can play it comfortably and speed it up later. Some people do get a reputation as being a "natural player." I don't know if there is such a thing. I think you have to work at it. When you hear something that intrigues you and you don't know if you can play it yet, it makes you listen more.

—PHIL SOUSSAN

Music is a language. When you speak it, it reflects your life.

—BILLY SHEEHAN

If you have the right temperament to keep it all together by holding down a groove and don't need to take solo after solo, then the bass is for you.

—STU HAMM

It's a weird thing when you are drawn to a certain instrument. It's a great mystery and we don't have any answers. I think it's something that the universe says to you in a moment of consciousness or unconsciousness. You should learn the bass because it's the instrument that speaks to you.

—KASIM SULTON

When I first started playing bass and practicing, it soon became apparent that the sound of the bass is that of one hand clapping. You need to play with other people, it's a bit pointless by itself. Quite quickly on, I met Steve and Paul from the Sex Pistols. I overhead they were looking for a bass player. They asked me, "Who's your favorite band?" I said, "The Faces." They said, "That's our favorite band too!" So the Faces song "Three Button Hand Me Down" was my audition song for the Pistols. It got me the gig. Many years later I actually got to play live with the Faces and we played that exact song!

—Glen Matlock

Introducing the Titans: #1–11

Titan #1: Victor Wooten

Victor Wooten relaxing with his bass.
Photo used with permission from https://www.victorwooten.com/press

Wooten is a five-time Grammy winner and a founding member of the supergroup Béla Fleck and the Flecktones. He has won every major award given to a bass guitarist, including being voted "Bassist of the Year" in *Bass Player* magazine's readers poll three times (the only person to win it more than once). In 2011, *Rolling Stone* magazine voted Victor one of the "Top Ten Bassists of All Time." https://www.victorwooten.com

I got so much great advice from the Victor Wooten Music Lesson book. I like the part when he asks, "If you could pick any historical figure to play with, who would it be?" and

then whatever the answer was, he would put on the CD and then say "go." That book distills any great teaching that anyone's taught me in a clean and pure way.

—Liam Wilson

Titan #2: Billy Sheehan

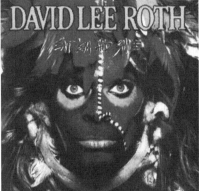

Billy played bass on David Lee Roth's *Eat 'Em and Smile* album (1986).

Billy Sheehan is a prolific bassist who has worked with Talas, Steve Vai, Mr. Big, and David Lee Roth. He has a trademark lead bass style and has won many awards such as "Best Rock Bassist." www.billy sheehan.com

We opened for Mr. Big in 1988. When we walked off the stage into the dressing room, the whole band was in our dressing room singing our song "Goldilox." They sang the whole thing with harmonies. We've been friends ever since. We are completely different bass players but I love what he does.

—dUg Pinnick

I was watching a VHS tape of Billy Sheehan. He was doing all these crazy tapping techniques. Then he said, "You can learn all these crazy tappings, but when are you going to use it, for maybe ten seconds in one song?" He then said, "Learn the basics before you learn all the hard stuff." That really stood out to me.

—Michael Lepond

I was amazed when I first heard Billy Sheehan on the David Lee Roth album Eat 'Em and Smile. *He rewrote the book on rock bass on this great album.*

—Davey Rimmer

Billy Sheehan is a monster. You watch him play a bass solo, and think, "that stuff's not possible."

—Stu Cook

Titan #3: Justin Chancellor

Justin Chancellor of Tool.
Photo by Travis Shinn

Justin Chancellor is best known for being the bass player in the band Tool since their 1996 studio album *Ænima*.

I'm impressed with Tool, especially their live stuff. Nobody is like them. Their music is murky and muddy and kind of prog-rock-for-now. It is so deep and well done. I like smart music. And it's awesome that Maynard named his son Devo.

—Gerald Casale

Tool are amazing! When I moved to LA, I stayed at Danny Carrey's house for three months. It was amazing how they waited thirteen years to release their latest record. When I was there, they worked every day and reworked that album a bunch of times. They have an amazing work ethic.

—Julie Slick

Titan #4: John Patitucci

John laying down the groove. Photo by Gus Cantavero

Acoustic and electric bassist John Patitucci has been at the forefront of the jazz world for the last thirty years and is a four-time Grammy Award winner. He has performed and/or recorded with jazz giants such as Dizzy Gillespie, Wayne Shorter, Herbie Hancock, Chick Corea, and many others. https://johnpatitucci.com/

I had to fill in for John Patitucci one time. Chick Corea asked me to sub for him in the electric band. I got to dive into the material. It took me hours and hours of dedicated practice. That really made me want to practice.

—Nathan East

I love John Patitucci. I love the earthiness and the bluesiness of his quote unquote jazz fusion playing.

—Bryan Beller

Titan #5: Geezer Butler

Geezer played bass on landmark Black Sabbath albums like *Masters of Reality* (1971).

"Geezer" Butler is most well known for being the bassist, songwriter, and main lyricist of Black Sabbath.

Geezer is a key bassist that I picked up early on. Black Sabbath is one of my all-time favorite music groups. Geezer is a big part of their sound.

—Chuck Dukowski

Geezer Butler has the great Jack Bruce "bending notes" style.

—Harley Flanagan

I still love the pioneers who are not virtuosos but are crucial pillars of music, like Geezer Butler.

—Armand Sabal-Lecco

Titan #6: Jeff Berlin

Jeff and his bass skills. Photo by Bruno Sappadina

Jeffrey Berlin is a fusion bassist who became prominent as a member of the band Bruford with Bill Bruford.

Jeff Berlin was a hero of mine.

—Bubby Lewis

One of my initial bass heroes was Jeff Berlin.

—Michael Manring

Titan #7: Ron Carter

Ron enjoying the bass.
Photo by Sophie LeRoux.

"Sir" Ronald Carter is a jazz double bassist who holds two Grammys. He has played on over 2,220 recordings and is the most-recorded jazz bassist of all time. https://roncarter.net/SirCarter/

Ron Carter was my first jazz bass hero. If you had fifty jazz albums, Ron Carter was probably on forty of them. People always get turned on by speed, but that's not why you get called for gigs. There was a reason why he dominated every jazz record he was on. He really understands what his role is as a bass player.

—Christian McBride

I grew up playing a lot of jazz, so Ron Carter was a major influence on me.

—Angeline Saris

Titan #8: Stu Hamm

Stu Hamm, bass man.
Photo by Richard Ecclestone

Having stunned audiences across the world with his innovative playing, Stu Hamm has made a name as the go-to bass player for the world's great musicians. His time spent playing with Steve Vai and Joe Satriani cemented his place among the greats and gave Stu the platform to display his pioneering bass techniques to adoring crowds worldwide. www.StuHamm.com

Stu Hamm is one of my biggest heroes ever. One of my first concerts in 1990 was going to see Joe Satriani at the Massey Hall in Toronto, when Stu was on bass. The show completely changed my life, no exaggeration. It's when I decided to be a bass player for a living. To record with Stu more than thirty years later is mind blowing. To have him also be a great guy too was just the icing on the cake.

—Jason Raso

Titan #9: Nathan East

Session Master Nathan East.
Photo by Rob Shanahan

Grammy nominated bassist Nathan East is credited on over 2,000 recordings and is recognized as one of the most recorded musicians in the business. He is known for his musical collaborations with Eric Clapton, Phil Collins, Quincy Jones, Michael Jackson, Ringo, George Harrison, BB King, Stevie Wonder, Anita Baker, and Daft Punk. https://nathaneast.com/

He produced my first solo album. He did some amazing work on all these pop songs on records that I loved, like Whitney Houston's "Saving All My Love For You." You could tell he has the chops and could go crazy but yet he always would play the coolest little riff just at the right spot. With his pocket and suggestion of things, he's a very gifted musician.

—Gail Ann Dorsey

Titan #10: George Porter Jr.

Friendly George Porter Jr. Photo by DLSMUSICPHOTO

George Porter Jr. is best known as the bassist of legendary New Orleans funk pioneers, The Meters. Porter is also the band leader of his own unique long-term projects, the Runnin' Pardners and the Porter Trio, in addition to a few exclusive performances exploring The Meters songbook with Foundation of Funk. Porter tours prolifically and continues to receive accolades on the jam band and festival scene. www.Georgeporterjr.com

I'm back to George Porter Jr. as being a major influence.

—Kinley Wolfe

George Porter was a major influence.

—Brad Smith

Titan #11: Verdine White

Verdine White has won six and received two honorary Grammy Awards. EWF has earned over fifty platinum/gold albums with over 90 million worldwide album sales. He is widely recognized as one of the 100 top bass players of all time.

Verdine White was a hero of mine.

—BLAISE SISON

Verdine White has played with Earth Wind & Fire since the band's inception in 1970.

Day 1: "Future Titan of Bass" Challenge Action Step

Thank you for participating in this challenge! As a special free treat, because I value each and every one of you, there are some free gifts to take part in! Please perform these three actions as soon as convenient:

1. Log on to http://www.bassguitarbeginner.com and register and sign up for the challenge.
2. Join the "Titans of Bass" Facebook group at https://www.facebook.com /groups/2548463212118457.
3. Visit "Titans of Bass" YouTube channel at https://www.youtube.com /channel/UCPTsxR-dP0_zGgKVaJ6SFpg.

Watch the "Titan Challenge Day 1" video. It's totally free to take part in this. I ask that you please subscribe to the channel, click "LIKE" on the video, and post a quick comment letting us know that you performed the daily task. In this way we can act like accountability partners for each other and feed off each other's energies!

Your 14-Day Roadmap of the "Titans of Bass" Challenge

This one is easy but important. Please go over the next fourteen days of your challenge so you can plan out your next two weeks of your amazing journey.

Day 1: Roadmap—Planning out your 14-day journey.

Day 2: Groovy Gear 1—The Bass-ics of buying a bass.

Day 3: Groovy Gear 2—Amp it up. *Visit the music store, obtain a bass, cord, and amp.

Day 4: Tuning time!

Day 5: String theory, memorize E A D G strings. Start plucking.

Day 6: The Titans of Bass special song! Listen to different versions of the song. Listen to the song with the bass notes. Keep plucking.

Day 7: Connect-the-Dots Adventure—Play Note #1: C. Listen to the song with the bass notes. Play C to get going.

Day 8: Play Note #2: F and Note #3: G.

Day 9: Practice chord changes: (1) F to C, and (2) G to C. Listen to the song with the bass notes.

Day 10: Practice the first verse all the way through on the song with bass notes.

Day 11: Practice first and second verse/chorus all the way through without bass notes.

Day 12: Practice the whole song. Listen to the song without bass notes in place. Plan to have a "mini-concert" on Day 14.

Day 13: Practice the whole song with the introduction, record yourself. Listen to the song with no bass notes in place.

Day 14: Your first live performance (small group—family friends)! You have made it! You are a "Future Titan of Bass"!

Like most things in life, the best way to master a new skill—like cooking, painting, and learning the bass—is to practice, practice, practice. The aim of the "Titan of Bass" challenge is to make this practice more enjoyable and, dare I say, fun! This is because if it doesn't feel like practice, then you are more likely to do it. I hope the wisdom of these Titans of Bass spurs you on to finish the challenge and become a "Future Titan of Bass"!

ᗞᴀʏ 2

Groovy Gear
The Bass-ics
of Buying a Bass

Getting Your Paws on Your First Bass!

Do you have a bass already? If so, great! If not, it's cool! That's what we are going to go over today.

Here is a recommendation: Days 2 and 3 both involve the possibility of you going to a music store to purchase a bass, amp, and cord. It may be the easiest course to purchase both at the same time. So plan to go to the music store or, if you are borrowing, plan to go tomorrow.

The Anatomy of a Bass

Tuning Keys

String Guide

Headstock

Nut

Finger Board

Neck

Frets

Strap Post

Strings

Pickguard

Pickups

Body

Volume control

Bridge

Output Jack

Bridge Saddles

The bass is set up very simply and logically. We are now going to go over the parts of the bass so we can soon start playing it. There are three sections or areas of the bass guitar:

1. The Head
2. The Neck
3. The Body

Let's go over each one.

Parts of a bass.

The Head

The head of the bass is called the headstock. It's where the string tuners are. The tuning keys are found on the left and tune the four strings. The string guide holds the strings in place.

The Neck

The neck is the long area where the frets are. The fingerboard is the name for all the combined frets and the boxes to show where your fingers go. Frets are the metal strips that divide the strings into different notes. You put your fingers halfway between the two frets. There are four strings from top to bottom that are G D A E.

The frets on a bass are like your GPS.

—BAKITHI KUMALO

The Body

The pickguard is usually made of plastic and protects the body from possible damage from using picks. The volume control is a knob that controls the volume. There is also a tone knob, which controls the tone. The output jack is where you plug in the cord that connects the bass to the amplifier. The bridge is the metal square that holds the strings at the bottom. The bridge saddles are the grooves that lock the strings in place. Pickups are devices that take the string's vibrations and change them into electric signals.

So that's the nuts and bolts of the bass guitar. Ninety percent of basses will have this basic equipment on them. The picture of the bass listed is the classic Fender shape; it will always be in style. They will probably still be making it in a hundred years.

So let's see about getting you that bass.

What brands are ok?
How much should I expect to spend?
Do I have to have the best bass in order to play well?

Here are your options:

Buy a new bass guitar or used bass guitar (garage sale, eBay, Kijiji).

Borrow one from a buddy.

Lease/rent one from a music store. This is not a bad way to try before you buy!

Make monthly payments for a new or used one from a music store.

I have lent numerous bass guitars to my friends for up to a year at a time. I have nearly thirty bass guitars. I always know where my friends are.

—Rob Ruiz

I want you to start playing bass, fall in love with it, and become the next Victor Wooten. But let's walk before you run. The last thing I want is for you to spend thousands on a bass and amp and not really be into it. So let's take it slow, one step at a time.

Let's Ask the Titans: What Bass Should a Beginner Start With?

Ibanez, Lakland Skyline, Nash are top-quality basses.

—Geezer Butler

Sire guitars make basses that are top quality at very reasonable prices. I own seven of them.

—Shem Schroeck

I would recommend an entry level Warwick bass.

—Anais Noir

I've had Music Man StingRays for years.

—Tom Griesgraber

You don't need the most expensive stuff. A lot of the basses that I am playing on stage are about $1,000.

—Pete Griffin

If you are young, start with a 4-string Ibanez Soundgear as the necks are smaller. The bass is a big meaty instrument to get your hand around, a lot more than a guitar.

—BRYAN BELLER

When you buy new, make sure you buy at a store with a good return policy just in case.

—BARRY ADAMSON

When you start, find a neighbor who has a bass lying around and ask if you can practice on it.

—TONY SAPUTO

I'm sponsored to play Lakland basses. They have really changed my playing and make me approach bass in a different way. It's also cool that Geezer Butler plays them. They are a bass that can be a future goal for a beginner, as they are expensive.

—JULIE SLICK

Buy used gear. Find someone who is getting out of it, has outgrown it, or has a lot of basses. The quality doesn't matter so much if you are a beginner. Buy one from Craigslist or from your musical community when people get rid of theirs.

—BRAD SMITH

Entry models from Yamaha and Ibanez are great.

—MIKI SANTAMARIA

I played a 5-string bass for a while. But you can be much more creative by just using four strings, so I went back to one.

—PHIL SOUSSAN

Thanks, Titans. Now for our most popular answer . . .

Fenders! They were the first ones to popularize the bass guitar. It was invented in 1950 by Leo Fender and sold way back in 1951! It was the first bass to gain attention and inspire all basses after it. The first model was a Precision Bass and they still make them today.

When I was a young guy, there were two listings for bassists at the music union.

There was one just called (1) "Bass" (standup bass) and (2) "Fender Bass." It was a new instrument at the time. The early Fender marketing campaigns promoted the bass as an instrument for guitar players to increase their income. If you bought one, you could play bass on recordings.

—ROB STONER

Most of the Titans agree: Fender is a decent place to start your bass journey.

One make of Fender came up in Titan interviews a lot. I should know—it's the bass that I love and now play every day. Here's what the Titans say.

I'm back to playing Fender Precision bass with no pedals through an Ashdown head and a barefaced cab. It's pure, straightforward, and so comfortable. The groove goes on and on. I love Fenders because I can play crazy chromatic runs that I couldn't on any other bass. I've always had issues with active pickups; every one I've owned has had problems. Just because a bass costs $9,000 doesn't make it good. I now ask myself, "Why did I ever stop playing Fender?" Fenders give my playing a real zip. I can focus on my playing, not on how it sounds. When it comes to choosing my gear, I tell them a basic Fender Precision. All I want are the two knobs—volume and tone.

—JAH WOBBLE

In the Sex Pistols days when we went to record the "Anarchy In The U.K." song, we had a new producer, Chris Thomas, help out. He asked me, "You all set? What have you got?" I said, "I got my Rickenbacker." He said, "Where's your Precision bass?" I replied, "I didn't bring it. But don't worry, I just put a brand new set of strings on it." He rather dejectedly said, "Oh."

I still have that Fender Precision bass. Currently it's on display at a museum in Liverpool. Sometimes you are travelling and it's not conducive to take a bass with you. No matter where I go in the world, when they ask me what to get for a bass, I say "Get me a Fender Precision bass." They are all the same, reliable, consistent and universal.

—GLEN MATLOCK

You don't need to spend a lot of money right now. Buy a $300 Fender Squier and Amp combo that will be great for a long time. They feel ok and you can even upgrade the pickups. When you look at all the records from the fifties to seventies, 90 percent of them made were Fender Precision basses. Even now they sound so good in the final mix.

When I started with Tower of Power, I had my Fodera. It never really seemed right. I actually went and got a Fender Jazz bass. It was just so much better and fit into the music better. I like simplicity, just a front and back pickup with two or three knobs.

—Marc van Wageningen

If you are really young, get a short scale bass, like a Fender Musicmaster or a Squier. Don't get anything fancy, just something with a nice tone. If you are fully grown, get a Precision bass. If you have small hands, get a jazz bass, the neck's thinner. Get something basic and classic, not something with active electronics and all the bells and whistles. All those great Motown basslines were all Precision bass and little amps. If you buy a good Precision bass, you will still be using that in forty years, even if you are a professional. It won't go out of fashion, and it will pretty much sound good in whatever genre of music you want to play. To me it's the best sounding bass.

—Ben Ellis

When I look at my students' development in bass playing, it gets to a point where I ask them, "Are you ready for a good bass yet?" There were these two kids that came into class with Ibanez basses. They played and played, but there was something missing. Their playing wasn't firm. Their sound wasn't there, it was too bassy and too trebly. They dropped those basses and bought two brand new Fenders, a Precision and a Jazz. As soon as they got the Fenders, they started playing more freely, with much more interest in the other musical elements. Their tone also changed. The basses they had before kept them from becoming who they really were as players. As soon as they got Fenders, they turned into the bass players they were supposed to be. It was amazing.

—Scott Thunes

I've always been a Fender guy. I now have a Fender endorsement. Eighty percent of the classic records that you hear have Fender basses on them. Get a Jazz bass or Precision bass.

—Jon Button

I keep going back to the same bass that I still have back when I was fourteen. It's not the best sounding but it's the best feeling bass that I own. It's a Precision Bass with Jazz pickups. Back in 1972 I wanted to get more of that sound and definition that Jaco would get. I went to the guitar shop and I told them I wanted to put jazz pickups at the bottom. I think I was one of the first guys to do that. Now you can get Fenders with that pickup selection called "PJ sets."

—WYZARD

I played guitar and keyboards before taking up the bass. Part of the reason that I started playing bass was because of Zappa. I heard Tom Fowler playing on "Echidna's Arf" and was blown away. I had no idea that a clumsy old bass could play that kind of stuff! I was a huge Zappa fan and dreamt of playing in his band. I was good at guitar, but I was no John McLaughlin with huge chops. The same thing applied to keyboards. I figured that the bass might be my best chance to get into the Zappa band, so I bought a Fender Precision bass and started practicing. A few years later my dreams came true and I was playing in the Zappa band!

—ARTHUR BARROW

I like the story of Geddy Lee from Rush. He was playing both the Rickenbacker and the Fender Jazz basses. He was trying to create specific sonic parameters that he applied to both instruments. In the end he felt more comfortable playing the Fender Jazz bass. It carried him on for the rest of his career.

—RUDY SARZO

I made the mistake of not getting my first Fender bass until 1983, after I was already playing for ten years. I didn't realize what the sound of the bass guitar truly was until I got one. It's a real guitar that I could use to make real music. My advice is to get a Fender Jazz or Precision bass. The Jazz bass has a thinner neck so it's easier to play if you are younger and smaller. Get the sound of those basses in your head as soon as you can. It's really the ground zero for the instrument, the true sound of bass.

—DANIEL MIRANDA

I've played a $500 Mexican-made Fender Bass live and on recordings since 2000.

—CHUCK DUKOWSKI

So, let's just say that Fenders are what we should look at.

How to Buy: The KISS System for Bass Buying

You can own two hundred basses in your career but when you pick any of them and play it, it will always sound like you. A lot of guys get misled into thinking that the bass is completely responsible for the tone you get. Your touch has just as much to do with it as the bass itself.

—Basil Fearrington

Buy one you can afford. It is not necessary to spend a lot of money to learn an instrument; once you learn to play great, that is what you want to spend the money on.

—George Porter Jr.

So we are going to aim for the basics: four strings, two knobs, and no active pickups. Active pickups means more wiring and more complicated designs. The simpler, the better.

Assuming you can't borrow a bass and amp from a friend and don't have one already, it would be a good idea to visit a music store to check out the new and used equipment. Even if we are going to buy used, or so forth, it's still a great idea to stop by a store to do some research and have the chance to check out some basses. Many stores have used/refurbed sections—these are great places to do "research." Plan to go tomorrow after we go over some information about amps.

Bass Research

It's recommended that we go to at least play the bass and touch it. Hold it in your hands.

How does it feel?
Does it feel comfortable?
Does it hurt to reach around to play the strings?
Try to pluck the open strings to see how it feels.
Is the neck too thick? Not thick enough?

Try five basses until you are able to feel which one is more comfortable. There is common wisdom that many Titans knew a bass was right for them the minute they tried to play it. There is something to this.

I'll pick up a bass and it works for me or it doesn't. The same thing with an amp. I can't change it. I think choosing the right instrument is more innate than anything.

—GUY PRATT

As long as you have a bass that is from a reputable brand, it's not so much that the bass is right, it's more that if it's right for you. If the bass "feels" right, it will be a lot easier to play. This might be tricky, as some basses might look really cool but might not be the most comfortable for you. Does the bass feel awkward to hold and play?

Be honest in your first impressions. Close your eyes and play the E string (the bottom string, the largest) with your fingers.

Sometimes a bass will feel wrong because its shape and size just aren't for you. Don't get pushed into buying a bass that isn't for you. You will know when the right bass is in your hands. Here is a quick and dirty checklist for choosing the right bass for you, whether new or used.

1. Right now you should think of the bass as if it was an applicant for a job; don't fall in love with it quite yet. If it's plugged into an amp, turn it down to zero. Pluck the strings and just listen.

2. It's true that the sound of the bass comes from the amp, but the bass should sound clean without amplification. To produce a clear sound, the build of the bass matters—the construction of the wood, metal, and plastic in the body, neck, and head of the actual bass.

3. Do your best to listen. See if you can hear any buzzes when you pluck the strings. The notes you produce should sound clean, not strange or off-sounding noises. Do you like the notes that you hear now, without amplification? Amplification will only make those notes or tones louder, it won't "change them" necessarily.

The sound of an electric instrument comes primarily from the actual instrument, not the electronics. You can usually tell if you have a good one without even plugging in.

—Chuck Dukowski

4. If you are strapped in, take the bass off the strap. Check out the surface, top to bottom—the neck, body, and head. Does the "finish" or paint job look good? Are there any cracks, dings, or uneven areas in the paint? Look closely at where the neck meets the body, the seams, and so forth.

5. For used basses, the state of how it is now can tell a lot. Is it trashed, dirty, and beat-up looking? These are all bad signs. If you notice any huge issues now, it might be time to reconsider another bass for purchase.

6. The "action" is how the bass actually plays, how the strings that are above the frets meet to create a note. It should sound good when you press the strings on the fretboard and it should be easy to play the notes.

7. Plug the bass into the amp with the cord. Put the strap back on it—there are two holders on the bass, one on top and one on the bottom. Turn up the volume on the amp and the bass to a quarter of its capacity so you can hear the bass clearly. Now we are going to go over playing some notes on each string. Pay attention to how "clean" the notes sound, and if you find the tone pleasant or not. Let's start with the G string, the smallest string on the "top" of the bass when you hold it horizontally. Press down on every fret, from 1 to 5, starting with your index finger on the first, your middle finger on the second, and so on. This way you can go through four frets each time with your hand. Press each fret firmly with your fingers as best you can. Can you hear any buzzing or weird off-tones? Make sure that all the frets sound good. Go through every note on the G string. See if there are any frets that sound different from the others. It may be an indicator that some frets need to be filed down. Continue this exercise for all four strings—the D string, the A string, and the big E string.

Once you've picked one out that you like, make sure you plug it in and see if you can get a decent sound out of it.

—Chuck Dukowski

8. Check out the knobs, tuners, tuning pegs. Do all the knobs flow smoothly when you turn them? Are the tuning pegs straight and lubricated? If it is new, everything should be tip top; knobs should be easy to turn and not crackle or make strange sounds when you turn them.

The time to "kick the tires" as it were, is right now, both for choosing and negotiating. If you uncover any major issues, then it's best to let the seller know right away. If it's a new instrument, you could ask for a deal or choose another instrument. Remember there are plenty of basses out there. If you know another bass player, it's a good investment to have them along with you to check it out.

Sometimes it's a good idea to ask for little extras to sweeten the deal, like a carrying case/travel bag, a few picks, a set of new strings, or a discount on an amp to be thrown in. A used bass should depreciate far less than new. If you buy wisely, it should retain its value very closely.

It's hard to go wrong with a Fender. Simplicity is important right now. The more basic it is, the less there is to go wrong. Sometimes a more expensive bass doesn't necessarily mean that it's better. Buy something classic that won't go out of style and that is versatile. At this stage, try out as many basses as possible. The more research you can do right now, the better.

Secondhand Basses: Worth a Second Look

I would look on Craigslist and eBay and see if you can get a bargain.

—MARK BEDFORD

When I started, I just bought any cheap stuff secondhand locally. A secondhand bass is usually only a problem if the strings are miles from the frets. Start playing. See if you like it. If you do, then look into buying a better one. People put too much emphasis on equipment; once you've got reasonable working gear the sound is in your fingers. Don't waste your time thinking you'll sound better if only you had new pickups. The reality is that you'll sound better if you practice more!

—CHRIS DALE

It's more important to be on your toes when you are buying used gear. You can't expect a private seller to have guarantees, and so forth, like a music store would.

It really is "buyer beware" or "as-is." Sometimes instruments can be neglected or abused and, like any machine, it's not a good idea to tackle these issues yourself.

Take the KISS principles listed above and also remember these extras. A lot of your consideration when buying used is to determine how well the owner cared for the instrument. Is the neck warped and curved? This is a bad sign, as it may not be fixable. Pass on these. The safe bet is to get a bass that hasn't been modified. Ask the owner if any have been performed. There shouldn't be a lot of reasons to modify a decent instrument.

It's ok if you walk away from buying a used bass that isn't up to snuff. It's your hard-earned money—spend it wisely. Do a quick check on Craigslist or Kijiji to see if the price is fair. Even if you have to look at other cities or states, it can serve as a guide. Also, if the price is far lower than others, ask yourself why? The instrument's problems usually don't get better as you get home and play it more.

Introducing the Titans: #12–20

Titan #12: Kasim Sulton

Kasim on stage. Photo by Jim Snyder

Kasim Sulton is an American bass guitarist, keyboardist, and vocalist best known for his work with Utopia.

Many of our Titans have their own signature basses. Here are some options to look at.

Titan #13: Jack Casady

Happy Jack! Photo by Barry Berenson

Jack Casady is an influential bassist known for his playing in Jefferson Airplane and Hot Tuna.

I started playing the bass when I was sixteen years old in 1960. I got a Fender Jazz bass the first year it came out. I've always dabbled in basses and electronics for instruments. My Epiphone bass is not a signature model, it's an actual Jack Casady bass. It's the only model in their line like that. This bass has been on the market for twenty-three years, which is amazing. I wanted to build an instrument that engineers would love in the studio. I built the pickups myself. Every new year when there is a new batch of them, I take two of the new instruments and play them on the road as is. I can take them out of the box and they sound like a jewel.

—JACK CASADY

Titan #14: Leland Sklar

"I am just so proud to be a part of the bass community!" Leland Sklar Photo by David Burgess

Lee Sklar is an amazing session player and live performer for over five decades. He's thought to have played on over 26,000 recordings!

One night I was working down at RCA Records. I had to drive down a record company basement recording studio for a project. Lee Sklar has played on it. They finished his bass part but lost the last half a minute outro of his bass. I knew his playing so I knew how he probably would end the tune. The producer told me to "Just be Lee for a minute." So I went for it. He gave me $1,000 for thirty minutes of work, and asked, "Is this good?" I said, "Yeah, we're good."

—Michael Dempsey

Lee is famous for the use of his "Frankenbass."

There's a lot of people that have modified instruments over the years. Sometimes you're really fortunate and the end results are better than the sum of parts. Other times, you plug in after and it could be the biggest stink ever.

—Lee Sklar

Here's what he has to say about bass modifications and the secret "producer switch." This is a strictly decorative switch meant to keep producers happy when he's recording.

It works. I could even be fooled by it. In your mind, you want to hear a certain change so you hear it when the switch is flipped. There's a certain mean-spirited quality to a producer's switch, but it seemed like a fun thing to do. Once in a while, if the guy keeps asking questions and you will spend half your day chasing nebulous requests, it's easier to have him see you flip the switch and change your hand position a little. There's a lot of times where my gig feels like I am a cheerleader and you want to keep the spirit of the session alive.

—Lee Sklar

Titan #15: Eva Gardner

Eva Gardner is a bassist from Los Angeles, California. She holds a degree in ethnomusicology from UCLA and has performed worldwide as the bassist for Pink, Cher, Gwen Stefani, Moby, Tegan & Sara, Veruca Salt, and The Mars Volta. www.evagardner.com

The Eva Gardner Squier bass is a really cool bass for a beginner. It has a good price point and the neck is a little smaller than a traditional Precision bass, like a Jazz bass. It might feel more comfortable in your hands. I recommend that if a beginner is younger, they should get a short scale bass, like a Fender Mustang. A Fender Precision is my go to, my home.

—EVA GARDNER

Eva and her Fender Bass. Photo by Bianca Buder

Titan #16: dUg Pinnick

dUg Pinnick is best known as the main songwriter, vocalist, and bass guitarist for the band King's X. https://www.dugnation.net/

Back in the day, King's X was on tour with Cheap Trick. Their bassist, Tom Petersson, always used a 12-string bass. I asked him what that was like and he handed it to me to check out.

It was really something special. Tom told me to get a hold of the creator of his 12-string, as they got endorsed. On the fourth King's X album Faith Hope Love *and on the* Dogman *record, I used a*

dUg Pinnick at your service.
Photo by Matt Kjorvestad

12-string on half those songs. Now I have my own 12-string signature by Schecter.

—dUg PINNICK

Titan #17: Adam Nitti

Adam and his bass. Photo by Frank Zipperer

Adam Nitti is an internationally celebrated bassist and recording artist whose last five instrumental solo albums have helped define his unique and innovative voice. https://www.adamnitti.com/

It was amazing to have something to offer from an instrumental perspective and play an instrument that's custom tuned for you. I have two different signature basses with Ibanez. I can take my ideas for customized instruments and have close relationships with a great company like Ibanez. It's absolutely an honor to work with them.

—ADAM NITTI

Titan #18: Scott Ambush

Scott Ambush in action. Photo by Brian Friedman

Bassist/luthier Scott Ambush is best known as the bassist for thirteen-time Grammy nominated contemporary jazz fusion band, Spyro Gyra. www.scott ambush.com; www.ambushbasses.com

In high school I attempted to build a bass but I never got to finish it. Early in the nineties, I decided to switch to a 6-string. This was when a big influence of mine, Anthony Jackson, had long been playing one. I was thinking of getting it built by Fodera, so I drove to the Brooklyn Fodera shop. I told them what I wanted, and they said that one they were building for Anthony would be done in a few weeks, and I could come back and check it out when it was completed. At the same time in the back of Guitar Player *magazine, I saw a review of a book by Melvyn Hiscock called* Make Your Own Electric Guitar. *I thought about ordering it.*

As I was waiting for the call from Fodera, I started exploring the idea of building one. I visited an exotic wood shop in Baltimore. The exact same book I was thinking of ordering was on the bookstand! I grabbed it and went to the counter. They told me that they didn't even order that book but the publisher had sent it to them with other books.

I used that book and reverse engineered some basses by taking them apart. I then built my first bass. Years later through social media, the author, Melvyn Hiscock, saw that I had posted about the book, and we are now Facebook friends.

—Scott Ambush

Titan #19: Roy Vogt

A Roy Vogt solo album, *Urban Legend*.

Roy is the first person to receive a master's degree in Electric Bass Performance from the University of Miami. http://www.royvogt.com/about-roy/

John Patitucci said something about a Yamaha 6-string bass that he designed. I wanted to have a bass that was designed by me too. Five years ago, Carvin (now Kiesel) approached me about doing a signature bass model. I wanted to make a good studio bass and different from anything else. Finally this is my sound!

—Roy Vogt

Titan #20: Stu Cook

Stu at the Palacio de los Deportes, Mexico City, Mexico. 2/27/2020
Photo by César Vicuña

Stu Cook is a founding member of Creedence Clearwater Revival (CCR), a member of the Rock & Roll Hall of Fame, and has been mixed up in the music business for over sixty years. From writing and recording to touring and studio production, he is a seasoned industry veteran. Cook, now retired, toured the world with his music project, Creedence Clearwater Revisited, for the past twenty-five years. The band earned a RIAA Certified Platinum award for its two-disc live album *Recollection*.

I play a Signature SC5 Stu Cook bass made by Mike Lull Custom Guitars.

The bass has a Fender Jazz style body and a pair of Gibson Thunderbird pickups.

It's a 35-inch scale 5-string with a custom designed Telecaster bass carbon fiber pickguard. I like the accessibility of the lower range notes not available on a 4-string.

—Stu Cook

Honorary Mention: Joe Osborn (August 28, 1937– December 14, 2018)

Joe played on famous albums like Simon & Garfunkel's *Sounds of Silence.*

Joseph Osborn was a revered member of the Wrecking Crew, a team that created most of the radio hits in Los Angeles in the sixties and seventies.

When I was twelve years old, I worked at my grandpa's potato farm. I had my transistor radio in a branch of a tree so I could hear it. I would listen to a lot of songs on the radio. I noticed Joe Osborn's bass playing. I thought to myself, "I want to do that, I want to play bass." Joe Osborn was my main influence. He never walked all over the singer when he played bass.

When I auditioned for the bass position with The 5th Dimension, they had me play at the Syracuse fair first. Joe Osborn used to play on all their records. I knew all his stuff. They offered to give me a book of his playing but I told them I didn't need it. I played that one gig and went on the road for the next four years with them.

—Michael Dempsey

My all-time favorite is Joe Osborn. He was so melodic. Sometimes he was busy but it never got in the way.

—Gail Ann Dorsey

The reason that I've included Joe here is that he was a legend, but also to illustrate that you can be a Titan of Bass and not rely on fancy gear and equipment. Here are some legends about how solid he was in his gear choices.

1. He was said to have never changed his bass strings during his fifteen-year career as an LA session player. Think of how many hits those strings played on!
2. He rarely changed his bass settings. Most of the tracks he played on have the exact same settings.
3. He supposedly only used one bass throughout his long career! He started with a Fender Precision back in 1958. He worked on some hit records so he became the proud owner of a 1960 Fender Jazz bass prototype that he ended up using on recordings for decades! He later tried another 8-string bass but didn't like it and went back to his dependable '61 Jazz bass.

There you have it, proof that you don't need the fanciest technology and a $10,000 bass with all the bells and whistles. Get yourself a Fender and start grooving!

Day 2: "Future Titan of Bass" Challenge Action Step

1. Visit http://www.bassguitarbeginner.com for Day 2 of the challenge.
2. Visit the "Titans of Bass" Facebook group (details in "How to Use This Book" section).
3. Visit the YouTube channel (details in "How to Use This Book" section).

Learn and decide what bass you might want to get. Can you borrow, buy used, lease, or buy new? Make some notes; send some emails on Kijiji or Craigslist inquiring about some adequate basses. Plan to visit the music store tomorrow to get a bass and amp—or borrow, rent, or lease one from a friend or from school as soon as possible.

ＤAY 3

Groovy Gear
Amp It Up

Much Ado about Amps

Do you have an amp already? If so, great! If not, it's cool! That's what we are going to do today. *Visit the music store, obtain a bass, cord, and amp.

As you know, we want to keep things simple. There are tons of amps available. A "practice" amp will suit us just fine now. You should be able to find a practice amp pretty easily. If you are playing live gigs you will want something bigger. There are two main types of amps:

1. Combo—self-contained with amp and speaker, very common. We will start here.
2. Stack—the head and the cabinet are separate. This is more elaborate and something we can look at later.

You will want a bass amp, not a guitar amp, as the low tones of the bass need some heavy duty speakers, and so forth. As we just want to get you started playing, we will just cover the basics.

Let's Ask the Titans: What About Amps?

I currently use Ashdown amps. Nowadays, there are hundreds of good amps for very good prices. Apart from the actual amp sound, reliability is most important. There is nothing worse than having your amp blow out when you are playing a gig.

—Geezer Butler

Any small combo with a single 15- or 12-inch speaker. Ampeg makes a great one.

—Justin Chancellor

Combo amps have come so far since I started out. I'd recommend anything by Fender Rumble. I love my Fender Rumble 2×10" 500-watt Bass Combo Amp. It's light, compact, and packs a huge punch.

—MARY HUFF

Get a good combo amp with at least 150 watts.

—BLAISE SISON

A Fender Rumble is a little powerful $100 amp that you could play in a room by yourself or in a garage band.

—TONY SAPUTO

Markbass makes great combo bass rigs. Check out the Marcus Miller CMD 101 Micro 60.

—SHEM SCHROECK

Anything by Ampeg is great, or Eden for a slightly different tone. If money is tight, maybe a Fender?

—TOM GRIESGRABER

I am an Ampeg Artist and I like a portable Ampeg combo. Be prepared to hold on to the small combo amp for learning, lessons, etcetera. The serious player will need a powerful amp when they play with their friends. I think of the guitar amps as sports cars and a bass amp as a semitruck. Bass frequencies are the very hardest sounds to properly reproduce and there is nothing a bass player can do to alter the laws of physics.

—STEVE FOSSEN

The old Fender acoustic amps were great . . . And of course Orange which I now use onstage. You must find an amp that has the sound you envision.

—SUZI QUATRO

Some small 30-watt combo amp. I'm endorsed by EBS. They make some great ones that I use for quiet practice. Other than that I would recommend an audio interface and some cheap software plugs, as you can start experimenting with different sounds early on.

—HENRIK LINDER

You only need a small amp to start out on. Fender makes some really good ones. Ampeg and Accoustic make some small combos that also work great.

—KINLEY WOLFE

For a beginning bassist, just find the nicest amp you can afford and one that you can lift. There are so many great amps available now. To practice and learn, any small combo will do—2×10s, 1×12, 1x15 (a favorite of mine); 15–30 watts or so will do nicely for your bedroom. You could get something like that new for $100–$200. You can do very well with a used amp. Especially if you're just seeing if bass is your thing.

—James LoMenzo

A practice amp is fine for playing at home by yourself but I reckon you need at least a 100-watt rig for playing in a group. You don't need to play loud but you generally have to compete with a drummer and your 5-watt practice amp is gonna be useless in that situation.

—Horace Panter

Buy nothing bigger than a 50-watt output as size and weight are the important factors. Try them out in a shop if you can. I use Laney, Ibanez, and Fender amps and any of these will work and last for many years.

—Dave Pegg

Get something that you can play along to the drummer with. You definitely want an amp that can be heard above a drum kit. Ampeg does this little bass kit, the B115, solid state amp with 115 in it. They're great—you can play bar gigs with them. They are little. If you can't afford Ampeg, get a 15-inch speaker transistor amp so you can feel the bass.

—Ben Ellis

Any kind of combo amp that doesn't color the sound too much and is affordable. Get a Fender or Ampeg combo amp. So many companies are making great amps these days. Don't be discouraged that it's not loud enough to fill Yankee Stadium. You want to hear every note that you play. You need to put yourself under a microscope, the sooner the better.

—Daniel Miranda

The amp is not that important. If you play with a band, you'll need to hear yourself when you play with drums, so go for an amp of 100-watt minimum.

—Miki Santamaria

Fender and Ampeg have great inexpensive combo amps that are fantastic for beginners.

—Oneida James

Amps also benefit from good quality. Get something that can get you loud enough to play in a small ensemble so you can jam with other people but that'll come down in volume enough to not blow out everyone in your building. I like Gallien-Krueger, Roland, Yamaha, Fender, Aguilar, Markbass amps.

—CHUCK DUKOWSKI

Once you know what bass you want, start plugging the bass in to different amplifiers to see what the tone quality is like, and decide which amp from there.

—RONNIE DAWG ROBSON

Get the best sounding little amp that you can; it needs to sound beautiful. Biofeedback is most critical for people just starting out. Each note can be a little symphony. The better it sounds to the player, the more irresistible and rewarding it will be to practice and play. I like Mesa/Boogies.

—STEPHEN JAY

I would start with a Kingston MTD and a GK [Gallien-Krueger] combo because as you grow in your playing and [your] understanding of tone grows, you'll want a great bass and amp.

If you already get some stuff that sounds dope, it'll save you the trouble of finding stuff later.

—BUBBY LEWIS

I grew up playing through headphones in my amp. A lot of the tone of the bass comes from your hands, not the amp so much. Get a good Fender bass and any kind of amp to plug into.

—JON BUTTON

A Peavey TKO bass amp is great and indestructible. Old Fliptop Ampegs, even the Chinese models in the '80s/'90s, sound amazing but are a little pricey.

—JD PINKUS

I like simplicity in my amps. I only want the big four—Volume, Bass, Treble, and Midrange. I don't want a whole EQ [equalizer] thing to mess with. Just keep it simple."

—MARC VAN WAGENINGEN

Make sure to get an amp with a headphone jack. Vox, Fenders, and Trace Elliot are all good. Ashdowns are a little pricier. Get a small practice amp. Practice is something that you don't want anyone to hear anyways.

—BRAD SMITH

The moral of the story? For your initial bass journey, it's important to budget properly. If you are on a limited budget, I would suggest purchasing a better bass guitar than amp. Don't get me wrong, you will need a decent amp, but your life will suck if you only own a crappy bass. The actual act of playing the bass is more important than amplification at this point. A used bass amp (as long as it works) if you purchase it wisely usually won't lose too much value. I've even made a few bucks buying and selling amps.

The Music Store

Get yourself to a music shop and pick up different basses and see which one feels comfortable to you. Get the shop worker to help you find something at the right price and the right fit for you.

—JOAN ARMATRADING

Purchase what you can afford since you can always upgrade later on. Go to a music store (hit them all if there is more than one in your area). Pick up various guitars to see what feels best in your hands.

—RONNIE DAWG ROBSON

As planned, now it's time to go visit a music store and to get a bass and amp for your journey. Remember everything we went over in the last two days and go for it!

Introducing the Titans: #21–31

Titan #21: Starr Cullars

Amazon Queen of Rock! Photo by Alina Papa Martinez

Starr Cullars is the CEO and major artist of Cosmic Nation Productions. The Amazon Warrior is the only female-musician-member of Parliament-Funkadelic; a major disciple of the late great Prince; and was named the Queen of Rock by rock legends Paul Stanley/Kiss; Sammy Hagar; Matt Sorum/Velvet Revolver; and Mark Hudson, Grammy producer. www.cosmicnationproductions.com

Exclusive: Titan of Bass Starr Cullars crashes Paisley Park to meet Prince: Part 1

I started playing bass in a bunch of neighborhood bands in college. In my senior year of college at Duquesne University, I sent some demos to Prince at his brand new Paisley Park Studios. I had a contact there named Eric Reid who went to my school. I had been pen palling them, trying to get my demos to Prince. I got a few rejection letters from the Paisley Park office that he was busy with family stuff.

I decided to drive out to Paisley Park myself. I drove from Philly to Pittsburgh to Minneapolis in the middle of a snow storm. I arrived there and camped out of the University of Minnesota in a boarding room. I found Prince's house which had a giant purple windmill in his backyard. His security guards told me how to get to Paisley Park.

I went there and waited in the parking lot and wrote several notes and left them in his car. The notes said: "Dear Prince, I drove 17,000 miles to give you my demo tape. Peace & love. Starr Cullars"

I would leave them on his car and seat until they chased us out of the parking lot a few times. Finally after three days of doing this, my friend Eric told me to come on in to Paisley Park. He said that Prince was in between doing some work with Miles Davis. He said I could come in and he would show it to me. Paisley Park was a palace; it was like heaven. I had a bass on my shoulder and a bunch of cassette tapes in my little bag. This was before iPhones and CDs and all that.

I went to confront Prince to give him my demos. His manager introduced him to me. He said, "This is a friend of Eric Reid. She's a bass player from Duquesne University." He said go ahead, you can talk to him for a few minutes. He left me there with him, shaking his hand and he's staring at me in shock, probably thinking: "Who is the girl with this bass guitar on running through my Paisley Park complex unknown and uninvited?"

He's totally tripping. He's trying to hit on me. I'm just trying to give him my demo tape. I say, "Look, I don't care if I'm not invited, you are going to take this demo tape." He said, "Listen, you have to give this to Alan Leeds upstairs. He's the president of Paisley Park. Then he'll give it to me." I said, "I'm not going through all that." He said, "Listen, you tell Alan if I don't get your demo tape tonight, I'm going to kick someone's butt."

I said "ok." I snatched my demo and ran up to Mr. Leeds' office. I told him what Prince told me to say, using the same language. He started laughing and said, "Honey, come on in." He sat down at his desk and opened up his top drawer. In his top drawer were all my little demo tapes. He said, "Oh is this you? We didn't know who you were." I said, "Yeah that's me." He said, "Ok, he'll get it tonight, come and sit down." The next night I got a call to audition with Prince, and the band at the time was Sheila Cecilia Escovedo, Levi Seacer, and Matt Fink.

I get there and I have my bass souped up. I'm nervous as hell because I realize after all this craziness, I finally get to play and meet him. Sheila told me to relax, it's going to be ok.

He comes in reading the same notes I left on his car! He's walking around me in a circle, when I'm on my knees holding my bass. He is saying: "Female, huh? Female bass player, yeah, I'm hard on my musicians." He's looking through the glass at my Italian roommate and says,

"Is that your boyfriend? Yeah, I'm hard on my musicians. I never had a female bass player. Are you sleeping with him? Yeah, I expect my musicians to do this and this, are you living with him?"

I got tired of his Gemini psychotic games so I stood up and I'm taller than him now. I backed him into the wall. He's holding his guitar, I'm holding my bass. I said, "Look, did you listen to my demo?" He said, "Yeah, I listened to your demo. I think you got a lot of talent and potential. I want to work with you. I got to finish this Lovesexy *album and then I will be ready for you."*

He put on his guitar, he said, "It's in B-flat," and he started playing. I started playing and the whole band started playing. Now I'm playing with my heroes and I'm tripping. Prince is beyond tripping. He's dancing around in my face, saying, "Ah female, female bass player, huh?"

He's soloing, he's on his knees, he's jumping around. Sheila's telling me to ignore him, just follow her. I'm playing, he can't believe it. He's tripping. Miles Davis then sends a call to the studio. A tech comes out and says, "Miles Davis needs you. He's at the airport."

Prince then runs out, throws his guitar in the air. A tech catches it before it falls on the ground. I'm like, "Oh my god." The whole band runs out. Then Sheila and Fink come back and say: "Well listen. He's got to go get Miles Davis, but Prince told us to keep playing with you."

I said, "Alright cool," so we kept playing. Sheila said, "Come on, let's talk." We are sitting and talking about being females in the music industry. She's telling me because of who she is and her family is, she has never had to audition ever in her life. She says she could never have done what I did. Prince was impressed. We are all impressed with you. Prince thinks you have a lot of talent. "He's going to call you tomorrow."

The next day he finally calls me and says, "This is Prince. I just wanted to thank you for coming. I think you have a lot of talent and potential."

I said, "Thank you very much for saying that. I know I busted into your complex."

He said, "No, I loved that about you. I'm not trying to tell you what to do, but you can come and stay with me while I finish and go out on the tour. Then I can get back to you and do your record."

We talked some more and he ended up propositioning me three more times in the exact same way. I knew he had a reputation for the women, even young women like me. I said: "Listen Prince, I am going to . . ."

. . . to be continued! So what happened to Starr Cullars? Did she go and stay with Prince until he was done with his album? Did they end up recording afterward? Stay tuned for part 2 later on. (How's that for a cliffhanger?)

Just for Fun! "More Cowbell!"

The amazing story of the revival of the
Blue Öyster Cult

Titan #22: Joe Bouchard

Joe from Blue Öyster Cult. Photo by Joan Levy Hepburn

Joseph Bouchard was the original bassist for the Blue Öyster Cult, playing on most of their hits.

Blue Öyster Cult was a stadium-sized band in the seventies and eighties, but by the nineties it had fallen out of favor. In 2000, Saturday Night Live *had to get a license to use the original recording of "(Don't Fear) The Reaper" when they released the famous "More Cowbell" TV skit. The band didn't know anything about the skit until they aired it.*

All of a sudden, the skit took on a life of its own. For the generations that missed us in the nineties, all of a sudden everyone was saying "More Cowbell!" It was fantastic! It breathed some new life into the Blue Öyster Cult! You can't even measure what it did to our catalog.

After people heard our most popular song, "(Don't Fear) The Reaper," they started checking out our other albums. Even right now, our catalog has great potential. We are still quite vital to a lot of people even though other bands from our era are forgotten. It was really a gift.

—JOE BOUCHARD

Titan #23: Wayne Jones

Wayne Jones and his gear. Photo by Mannix Photography Melbourne

Australian premier bass player Wayne Jones is a multirelease recording artist, writer, and producer. He has charted on USA and European smooth jazz radio stations. Wayne is also the CEO and owner of the Dim & Dimmer recording label and manufacturer of Wayne Jones Audio and Jones-Scanlon industry-awarded high-end bass amplification and studio monitors. https://www.waynejonesaudio.com/

When I was a teenager, I couldn't afford another bass cabinet, but my dad was a wood machinist and we built a cabinet. I was doing a clinic for Trace Elliot and Status basses here in Australia and became their product advisor. I was always curious about getting certain sounds out of the equipment. I asked them one day to do something with a design I had and they did.

I went to a speaker manufacturer called Lorenz Audio and we wired and designed it. It had a studio sound with a fast, powerful attack.

In 2001 it was acclaimed by Bass Player *magazine as one of the best in the world. Then September 11th came out and took out my orders. I kept playing and recorded CDs with a friend who invested in CDs. He wanted me to design him a cabinet as well as an*

amp. Once again they were acclaimed and well-reviewed. It all started from necessity, passion, and experience.

—Wayne Jones

Titan #24: Abraham Laboriel

A true bass titan. Photo by Scott Shepard "Shepardphotography"

Born and raised in Mexico City to Honduran (Garifuna) parents, he received his earliest training from his father, a gifted composer and guitarist. Abraham has played on over 4,000 known recordings. *Guitar Player* magazine has called him "the most widely used session bassist of our time."

I still love the pioneers I loved as a kid for what they did and which was never challenged, only accelerated—like Abe Laboriel.

—Armand Sabal-Lecco

I love Abe Laboriel's playing.

—Oneida James

Abraham Laboriel was a big influence on me—in my top five of all time.

—Scott Ambush

Titan #25: Neil Jason

Neil Jason is a professional bassist, producer, and composer. He has worked with Paul Mc-Cartney, Billy Joel, Roxy Music, Mick Jagger, Pete Townshend, Paul Simon, Kiss, Michael Jackson, Diana Ross, Celine Dion, Dire Straits, Eddie Van Halen, and John & Yoko to name a few. Neil Jason is also the co-owner and co-founder of Seamoonfx and Manhattan Prestige Basses. Neil Jason plays Manhattan Prestige Basses. https://neiljason.com/

Neil Jason shows us how to groove.
Photo by Iain Reid (Beanotown Photography)

Titan #26: Mike Watt

Michael Watt is a bassist and co-founder of the Minutemen. When Watt took up playing bass, it was largely to keep him and his new best friend (D Boon) off the sketchy streets of Pedro. http://hootpage.com/hoot_wattbio.html

Mike Watt is a legend and an amazing human, one of my favorite bassists. He is very down to earth and approachable but also incredibly intellectual. He is like a punk rock scholar. There's not too many people like that.

—Sean Lennon

I remember Mike Watt when he played with his band fIREHOSE. They toured with us when I was in the Butthole Surfers. I was a huge fan and amazed by his style.

—JD Pinkus

Mike Watt: A true original.
Photo by Mike Watt

Titan #27: Sean Lennon

Sean Ono Lennon has recorded on over a hundred albums and scored six films. In 2009, he started the label Chimera Music in his New York City kitchen. He has recently performed and recorded with artists including Miley Cyrus, Mark Ronson, Lady Gaga, Lily Allen, and the Flaming Lips. He is the son of John Lennon and Yoko Ono. www .chimeramusic.com

Sean Lennon: Bassist, producer, artist.
Photo by Charlotte Kemp Muhl

Titan #28: Bakithi Kumalo

Bakithi Kumalo is a South African bassist who is most known for playing live with Paul Simon for decades. He has also played with Joan Baez, Cyndi Lauper, Herbie Hancock, Tedeschi Trucks Band, Randy Brecker, Grover Washington Jr., and Mickey Hart.

Bakithi and his bass.
Photo by Bakithi Kumalo

Titan #29: Christian McBride

Christian McBride is a six-time Grammy Award winning bassist/composer and the host of NPR's *Jazz Night in America*. https://www.christianmcbride.com/

Ray Brown was in an amazing trio with Christian McBride and John Clayton. Hearing those three together as a power trio makes me want to get my butt in check.

—Tony Saputo

The always classy Christian McBride.
Photo by Anna Webber

Titan #30: Kai Eckhardt

Kai Eckhardt is a Liberian-German bassist-composer known for his work with the John McLaughlin Trio and the band Garaj Mahal, which he co-leads to the present day. https://kaieckhardt.com

I have my preferred bassists. These are the real bass players as opposed to all the others. Kai Eckhardt is one of these.

—Hansford Rowe

Say hi to Kai.
Photo by Kai Eckhardt

Titan #31: Michael Manring

Michael Manring striking a pose. Photo by P. Lissart

Michael Manring is a Grammy nominated bassist and composer who is best known for the innovative approach which he has developed over hundreds of recordings and thousands of performances throughout the world. www.manthing.com

Day 3: "Future Titan of Bass" Challenge Action Step

1. Visit http://www.bassguitarbeginner.com for Day 3 of the challenge.
2. Visit the "Titans of Bass" Facebook group (details in "How to Use This Book" section).
3. Visit the YouTube channel (details in "How to Use This Book" section).

Get yourself to a music store to check out amps and basses. If you are buying both the bass and amp together, make sure to try them both out at the same time. You want them to sound good together. It may be easier to get a deal if you buy both together. Do some research on new or used prices online. Make some notes, send some emails on Kijiji or Craigslist inquiring about some adequate basses and amps.

Ⓓay 4
Tuning Time!

You Can Tune A Bass, But You Can't Tuna Fish

Time to tune! It is true that the bass typically stays in tune longer than a guitar, due to the larger strings. Although when you have new strings or travel with it, or play the strings aggressively, you may need to tune it repeatedly. It's always a good idea to tune frequently. If you don't and one string goes out of tune (which one string typically does), your playing will sound off, no matter how you play. If you have the strings perfectly in tune, you will increase your chances of sounding good.

So Let's Tune!

There are a few ways to tune. We are going to practice our "ear," which means we are going to play some tones and try to match those tones to our bass strings. Training your ear is a valuable skill to learn. However, it will take some practice.

Before we start, go to the "Titans of Bass" YouTube channel and look at Day 4. Get the "Titans Tuning Video" loaded up and ready to go.

Top Secret Titan Tuning Trick!

Bass Titan Stu Cook (CCR) shares a secret tip to help us tune:

Steve Cropper from Booker T & the MGs taught me this. It's very simple. Start by tuning the G string first and go up from there (instead of tuning the E string first). The G string has the most tension. If you tune the G first, the neck is more stable; the other strings won't change the tension as much. There should only be minor tweaks after you tune this way.

—Stu Cook

So let's try out this Secret Titan Tuning Trick.

1. Grab your bass, amp, and cord.

2. Make sure the guitar cord is plugged into your bass on one end and plugged into the "input" jack of your amp.

3. Make sure the volume dial/knob on the amp is turned down.

4. Make sure that your volume knob on your bass guitar is turned down. Most basses have knobs; turning it downward usually means lowering the volume.

5. Turn on the amp. Click the "on" button. Most have a red light or other visible sign.

6. Gradually turn up the volume knob on the amp. Turn it up about 20 percent.

7. Gently strike the E string to see if you hear anything.

8. Gradually turn up the volume knob on your bass guitar. Do you hear anything? The E string should have a low, loud sound. Make sure that the volume is at a comfortable level. Now that your bass and amp are live, we can begin to tune.

9. Visit the YouTube channel Day 4 to hear the online bass sound tuner. As per the Titans' secret tuning trick, we are going to start with the top G string.

10. Look at the small G string on the top when you place the bass on your lap. Trace the string up to the neck, and find the tuning knob on the head area. Queue up the Titan tuning video on the YouTube channel and play the first video—G tone. You will find that turning the knob one way makes the string tone go "up" and turning it the other way will make it go "down." Gently pluck the string and listen to the sound that comes out of it. Turn the peg until you match the sound. This may take a little while, so feel free to play the video again.

11. Repeat the process: Locate the next string, the D string, the larger string one down from the G string. Queue up the Titan tuning video on the YouTube channel and play the second video—D tone. Gently pluck the string and listen to the sound that comes out of it. Turn the peg until

you match the sound. This may take a little while, so feel free to play the video again.

12. Repeat the process: Locate the next string, the A string, the larger string one down from the D string. Queue up the Titan tuning video on the YouTube channel and play the third video—A tone. Repeat the process: Gently pluck the string and listen to the sound that comes out of it. Turn the peg until you match the sound. This may take a little while, so feel free to play the video again.

13. Repeat the process: Locate the last string, the E string, one down from the A string. Queue up the Titan tuning video on the YouTube channel and play the fourth video—E tone. Repeat the process: Gently pluck the string and listen to the sound that comes out of it. Turn the peg until you match the sound. This may take a little while, so feel free to play the video again.

14. It's a good idea to go back to the G string and tuning video to see how in tune the G string is now.

15. I recommend getting a good electronic tuner to make this process a little easier. Look on the YouTube channel for recommendations under the Day 4 video: "Bass Tuners."

Let's Ask the Titans: When's the First Time You Noticed the Bass in Music?

I first picked out the bass notes on my 6-string guitar. I realized that this was what I wanted to do with my life.

—Leo Lyons

My brothers had me playing very early in life, but I don't remember the exact moment. When I was five or six we did a tour opening for Curtis Mayfield.

—Victor Wooten

Back in the sixties, a bass player named Joe lived around the corner from my house. I would have to go to bed early but I could hear the bass coming through the door. It was like when you hear a car's subwoofer off in the distance. I started playing soon after this, at age twelve.

—Billy Sheehan

As a kid probably around two or three years old. It was the low end of a ceremonial drum.

—Armand Sabal-Lecco

I always knew what the bass sounded like. My oldest brother played bass. I wanted to play drums when I was younger. But when I heard the solo Tom Kennedy took on "Synergy" on Dave Weckl's Synergy *album, it changed my life and view.*

—Bubby Lewis

I was maybe seven years old when I first noticed bass prominently in a song. The intro to "Brick House" by The Commodores is one of the earliest that I can recall.

—Shaun Munday

Back in the day I was a dog walker and I used to listen to the tapes in my Walkman. My brother made me a tape with the song "Walking On The Moon" by the Police. It rocked my world. I heard the first two notes and I was hooked. The bass was prominent without showing off. Hearing this song was the first time that I knew I wanted to be a bass player.

—Pete Griffin

I have a vivid memory of loving the guitar/bass riff in the Ray Parker Jr. "Ghostbusters" theme song from the first movie.

—Tom Griesgraber

I saw the Beatles on the Ed Sullivan show on their famous Sunday night appearance. I was smitten. At that time I was already very good at classical violin. The violin never had a chance when I saw the Beatles perform.

—Jeff Berlin

I remember seeing Bill Haley and the Comets on TV. Bill Black played a string bass on "See Ya Later Alligator" and "Rock Around the Clock." In 1964 I switched from piano and rented a Fender P bass.

—Stu Cook

I believe it was listening to "Stray Cat Strut" by Stray Cats . . . after hearing it I couldn't get the descending walk of the bassline out of my head!

—Justin Chancellor

I was listening to classical music when I was three or four years old. Bass was the dramatic part of the orchestra. I grew up in Washington, DC, so I went to a lot of concerts.

—JACK CASADY

I was always very percussive-minded when I was young. My first instrument was the bongos, then piano. I played percussion in my school orchestra. We had lots of family trips in the car with long distances. We were a musical family so we sang a lot of songs. I think it was in my DNA.

—SUZI QUATRO

When I was five years old, I heard the Barney Miller *bassline on TV. It became a joke of what bass players do to show off the funky bassline. We were all being drawn to the same very prominent bassline.*

—MARK STOERMER

I'm not too sure, as my family only had a cheap record player with a tinny sound. Only the songs with prominent basslines really stood out. I remember: "My Generation" by The Who, "Gimmie Some Lovin'" by the Spencer Davis Group, and "Under My Thumb" by the Rolling Stones.

—GEEZER BUTLER

It was funny, I saw a bass before I realized what it was. I played a guitar in bands in early middle school. There was a band that was playing at the dance school with a jazz bass. It had four strings. I thought it was an electric ukulele. The first time I really paid attention was the mid- to late sixties with McCartney's melodic parts.

—KLAUS FLOURIDE

I started out playing guitar. I basically picked things up by listening to the radio in the mid-1960s during the British invasion revolution. I joined and had to play bass to be in the band. It was explained to me that I needed to pick out bass in songs. Once I honed in on bass, I realized that I was already applying the fundamentals in how I played guitar and also being melodic.

—RUDY SARZO

I was maybe four or five and my parents had this floor model radio. It was a huge cabinet that was about four feet high with tuning knobs and tubes. I still remember hearing a Tex Ritter song called "Ghost Riders in the Sky." I remember bopping to it and holding onto the radio. I was tuning into the bass and really resonating with it.

—GERALD CASALE

I noticed at a show when there was another dude on stage who wasn't playing a guitar.

It seemed like it was a guitar with a really long neck. I reverse engineered it by looking in the credits of an album. I guessed that the guy was the bass player but I didn't really understand what it was. Later I heard the [Red Hot] Chili Peppers and the Suicidal Tendencies and their songs had this kind of slappy bass. It grabbed my attention, for better or worse.

—LIAM WILSON

I noticed the bass pretty early on, from listening to Kiss, AC/DC, Judas Priest where the bass was prominent and powerful. Most of my friends picked up the guitar or drums. It was interesting to me that nobody picked up the bass. My friends had a punk band, I'd watch the bass player. I liked how he played one note at a time. It seems mysterious to me. I thought, "I want to do that."

—BJORN ENGLEN

It was on the Damned's first album, the song "Neat Neat Neat." The first time I heard that on the record I thought, "What is that?" It seemed that the person given the bass was always the least musical of the group. I thought if I played the bass well that it could be my way into bands and music. There were never any good bass players around. I got my first bass when I was fourteen or fifteen. I knew the bass was for me.

—BEN ELLIS

It was in 1957 when I was five years old. My cousin brought this record home. We would play them when people came around. I heard a 78 recording called "Why Do Fools Fall In Love?" by Frankie Lymon and The Teenagers. It had a great bassline, I will never forget it. From that day on I became obsessed with the bass, I heard the bass in everything. I went around pretending to play the bass on a broom.

—dUg PINNICK

One memory that is seared in my brain was riding in my dad's car listening to Motown music when I was growing up in Brooklyn in the sixties. Hearing two particular tunes pushed me toward the bass. They were: "I Was Made To Love Her" and "For Once In My Life" by Stevie Wonder.

—JOHN PATITUCCI

The first time I was aware of the bass guitar was on the first LP that I ever purchased. I was learning to play the guitar and Hank Marvin was my hero. There was a track called "Nivram," or "Marvin" spelled backwards. When I switched from guitar to bass I would play along with it.

—DAVE PEGG

My dad was the bass player in the British band called "The Creation." I grew up hearing the bass, it was always on my radar.

—EVA GARDNER

My dad collected a lot of guitars and my brother had a drum set. When I was ten, I would mess around with the guitar. It never really spoke to me, I would fumble around with chords. When I was eleven, I looked at the only bass in my dad's collection, a fretless Gibson. I thought it would be easier; there were only four strings and I wouldn't have to learn bar chords. Later we went to the salon and the owner and stylist was a bass player. He realized that he was a bass player because he always noticed the basslines in songs. That was a light bulb moment for me. I was eleven when I started playing the bass.

—JULIE SLICK

I didn't notice the bass until I started to play it in a band when I was fourteen. The band on the block where I lived had two guitar players. They say you can be in the band but we need a bass player, not another guitarist. I didn't want to turn them down, so I was willing to sell the guitar and become the bass player.

—KASIM SULTON

When I started the Alice Cooper band with Alice, we didn't know what instruments to play. We met in art class in high school and we knew that we wanted to start a band and incorporate our artistic ideas in it. Glen Buxton was in our band and he could play the guitar. *The very first show that we did, Alice and I were pretending to play guitar and sing. It was funny because Glen was the only one actually playing guitar.*

The show went well so we decided that we were going to be a real band. By then everyone had already picked their instruments before me, so I was left with the bass. At that time I couldn't distinguish the bass on records because my home record player was so cheap. I would go to Glen Buxton's house and we would sit in his living room and play records. All of a sudden I could actually hear the bass. He showed me where the notes were on the neck. He told me that the most important thing was the feel of the song. He would play Rolling Stones or blues songs and he would help me figure out the blues patterns.

—Dennis Dunaway

My dad was a math teacher, so I think a lot of bass patterns I learned could be related to that. Certain people are drawn to the bass. Many times the bass player is just a frustrated guitar player. The bass has an important role holding a melodic groove. The bass has to be like the drum, everything shifts with the choice of bass notes. I get a lot more feeling and have the chance to move a lot more people with the bass. I now play banjo a lot, and it has really changed my bass playing.

—JD Pinkus

It started when my brothers were playing in the Christ the King church band in San Diego. One day when I was fourteen, I noticed the bass on the altar. I picked it up and started playing it and it felt comfortable. I was listening to Motown and James Brown and I focused on the bass subconsciously. I played cello from eleven to thirteen, so I had knowledge of the bass clef. The cello was tuned in fifths but the bass was tuned in fourths. So it was a little hard to play both at the same time. When I switched to bass, that was it for me. The bass player in my school band, Gunner Bigs, was a friend of mine. He was a great player. I would sneak in and memorize his bass parts. One day he was sick. I jumped in because I knew all the parts. When you get bit by a bug, that's it.

—Nathan East

I grew up in central Wales in the sixties. From 1960 to 1962, rock and roll bands played in England. There was something about the low end that appealed to me. At age fourteen or fifteen, I decided I would like to have a go on it. I was intrigued and amazed by it.

—Percy Jones

I have been into music since I was nine years old. In orchestra class I noticed the upright bass. I was immediately struck by it. I started taking lessons on it and the bass guitar at the same time.

—Verdine White

My father told me that when I was two years old, I stood in front of the radio and pretended to conduct the music. That was weird because I never seen anyone ever do that. So at age two, I have the intuition of music built in me. My dad was a singer and an active member of the musicians and artists associations in Mexico City. When I was six, I started on classical guitar. I gave it up at eight because it was too hard to play classical guitar chords as I had no fingertips on my index fingers. My brother then joined one of the most successful rock and roll bands in Mexico. All the publishing companies would send him all the songs for him to play in Spanish. The ones he didn't like he would give to me to check out. I was suddenly listening to the most incredible songs. I played along to those records by ear. The very first chord I learned was a D major chord. I learned the D and the fifth, how the remaining fingers would play the chord. I knew that one was representing the bass note. So I had an understanding right off the bat.

—Abraham Laboriel

When I first took guitar lessons around eight years old, I learned there were basslines, chords, and melodies. My first exposure to a bass player was Benjamin Francis. He was a gentleman that lived by me and became my informal mentor and teacher. He played bass on an acoustic guitar with just four strings on it.

—George Porter Jr.

I actually remember being very young and not knowing what the different instruments were. I remember loving music and when I first started to pick out guitar, drums, and bass. It was a real revelation. It's when I started getting into becoming a musician.

I kind of envy my childhood when I could just hear music without analyzing it in that way. When I make music myself—like mixing, producing—I can't shut off the analytical side of my brain. Bass was my first instrument that I played consistently and in a professional setting.

—Sean Lennon

When I was twelve, I started to mess around with my uncle's bass. One time I got drunk and I told him that I could play it. My uncle trusted me and said I could play it. Even though I was messing up at a concert, I was on the right track as a musician. Growing up in South Africa, I would look for bands to play with in local communities. Eventually they let me play.

—BAKITHI KUMALO

The Shadows was the first band I ever saw. I was drawn to looking at the bass even though they had a very famous lead guitarist. I liked the bass because it was a bigger instrument.

—BRUCE THOMAS

Just for Fun!

Devo: Inventors of music videos?! It's true!

We used to make music videos before there was even a name for it, shooting on 16mm film. We thought that this was what our career was going to be, making collections of short films with our songs driving the narrative.

We wanted to be the Dadaist Three Stooges using our music. We were also going to be the first multimedia band to release our materials on LaserDisc. Popular music and magazines were predicting that laser discs were right around the corner way back in 1974!

But we were sold a bill of goods. They had three competing companies creating three separate laser disc playing systems that weren't compatible with each other. This ruined the marketplace and it would be ten years before anything really happened. Although they were quite impressive with images and sound quality, it never really took off. Finally, more affordable DVDs came out and took over.

—GERALD CASALE, DEVO

Just for Fun! Don't Try This at Home!

Zany Zappa Zingers: Scott Thunes and his first gig with Frank Zappa

I was a young kid when I first started playing with Frank Zappa. Frank had been pushed off the stage in Rainbow Theatre in London back in 1970. From that point on, he hired a bodyguard named John Smothers. Our first gig was at the U of C in Santa Barbara.

For some reason, John wasn't around at the time. We were getting ready to play and I was standing next to Frank.

I got so excited that I hopped on Frank's back and slammed both of my hands down on both of his shoulders. I was so excited that I was about to go on stage with Frank that I physically attacked him. I mean, the reason I've been playing my music was to play on stage with Zappa! He turned around as angry as I've ever seen him and replied, "Never, ever do that again!"

This wasn't the greatest way to start my career. But it was fairly indicative of how I was at the time—I was a big hugger.

—Scott Thunes

Introducing the Titans: #32–40

Titan #32: Hadrien Feraud

Hadrien Feraud in black and white. Photo by Sandra Billaud

Hadrien Feraud was born in August 1984 in Paris, France. From 2002 to present, he has recorded and performed with many renowned musicians such as: John McLaughlin, Chick Corea, Jean Luc Ponty, Gino Vannelli, Jada Pinkett Smith, Thundercat, Billy Cobham, Dave Weckl, and many more.

Hadrien Feraud has demonstrated the highest ability to play music on a bass guitar that has ever been seen on planet earth, technically and harmonically.

—JEFF BERLIN

He has all the chops and he's also very musical. I wish that I lived in LA. I would actually love to take a bass lesson from him.

—MARC VAN WAGENINGEN

Titan #33: Bill Laswell

Bill Laswell: Bass, the Final Frontier. Photo by Yoko Yamabe

Bill Laswell is a visionary bassist and a two-time Grammy Award winner who has put his inimitable stamp on over 3,000 recordings and thousands of live performances. He has established his producer credentials working with Mick Jagger, Peter Gabriel, PIL (Public Image Ltd), Yoko Ono, Iggy Pop, and more.

We were lucky enough to have Bill to mix an album for us. He was our wishlist mixer.

—COLIN EDWIN

Titan #34: Percy Jones

Percy Jones and his fretless bass. Photo by Avraham Bank

Percy Jones is best known as a bassist of the jazz fusion band Brand X.

Percy Jones from Brand X was an influence when I was starting out.

—Kai Eckhardt

Titan #35: Leo Lyons

Leo Lyons and his beloved bass. Photo by Arnie Goodman

Leo Lyons, bass player, Woodstock legend, and founding member of Ten Years After. www.leolyons.org

Titan #36: Gail Ann Dorsey

Gail played bass on David Bowie's 1997 album *Earthling.*

Gail Ann Dorsey is best known as David Bowie's bassist from 1995 to 2016. She has also played with Lenny Kravitz, The National, Bryan Ferry, Boy George, Gwen Stefani, and many others.

Gail Ann Dorsey is an incredible player.

—JOAN ARMATRADING

Bowie always had tremendous bass players, like the amazing Gail Ann Dorsey.

—MARK BURGESS

Titan #37: Horace Panter

Horace, the bassist and artist. Photo by Sally Crane

Horace Panter is the bassist and co-founder of the British ska band, The Specials, and a professional artist, thereby inhabiting two occupations simultaneously!

Titan #38: Suzi Quatro

I am a bass player, not a failed guitar player, and that's why I don't use a pick. Bass and drums are the engine that drives the band. Everything else is colors. I take my job seriously . . . when I lay it down, I lay it down and always make sure it's "in the pocket." And this, folks, is the bass-ics of bass playing. http://www.suziquatro.com/

—Suzi Quatro

The first time I noticed the bass as an instrument was watching German TV in 1973 before I even played. It was Suzi Quatro playing the song "48 Crash."

—Kai Eckhardt

Suzi Quatro—bass legend.

Titan #39: Dave Pegg

"I am honored as a folk-rocker to be in this book!"
Dave Pegg
Photo by Kevin Smith

Dave Pegg is a bassist and the longest-serving member of Fairport Convention and also with Jethro Tull. www.davepegg.co.uk

Titan #40: Billy Gould

Billy played bass on all the Faith No More
albums, such as 1989's *The Real Thing*.

Billy Gould is the bassist of Faith No More. He also runs an independent label
called Koolarrow Records. https://koolarrow.com/

Day 4: "Future Titan of Bass"
Challenge Action Step

1. Visit http://www.bassguitarbeginner.com for Day 4 of the challenge.
2. Visit the "Titans of Bass" Facebook group (details in "How to Use This
    Book" section).
3. Visit the YouTube channel (details in "How to Use This Book" section).

Tune the bass so we can get started playing it and practicing. This might seem
tricky at first, but it's a valuable and needed skill. Take your bass and practice tuning it with your ear. Think about investing in an electronic tuner. Go
through the steps of tuning your bass.

Day 5
String Theory, Memorize E A D G Strings, Start Plucking

Note Time

Now that we are tuned up, let's do a little work and go over some notes.

Knowing where the notes are is one of the most important skills that you can develop in your career as a Titan of Bass. Think about the bass instrument as a way to communicate with the other musicians you play with, or any of your listeners, via a message of music. Knowing the note locations and names is a plus, as when you read music it will all correspond.

Strings: E A D G

Let's start with the open strings. We are going to focus on the 4-string bass as it's the most common and you can do 90 percent of all styles and songs with it.

E: On the bottom, when you are holding it to play, is the E string. It's the largest string.

A: The A string is above the E string, and it's the second largest string.

D: The D string is above the A string and it's the third largest string.

G: The G string is at the top, above the D string, and it's the thinnest string.

E A D G Made Easy

It's a great idea to memorize the strings! This will make it easier to get used to the notes and tones that you want to play! Pick one that you want to use!

Here are some ways to remember the string letters by using clever acronyms (the first letter of every word in the phrase) containing the four string names: E A D G.

Eddie Ate Dynamite. Good
Elephants Always Do Good
Eat A Dead Goat
Every Adversary Dies Gloriously
Eat At Dan's Grill
Eat Another Donut, Gary

Which one do you want to use?

The Rest of the Notes

You now know the four open string notes are E, A, D, G. The good thing is there are only seven letters in total in the musical alphabet!

A B C D E F G: These seven tones have semitones in them, basically meaning the half steps in between them. To illustrate, we have A, A-sharp, B, B-sharp, C, C-sharp, D, D-sharp, E, E-sharp, F, F-sharp, G, G-sharp. A sharp note can also be called as the flat of the higher octave. So an A-sharp is also a B-flat.

In the interest of simplicity, let's call everything a sharp instead of a flat. There is no right answer to this, it's just choosing one method that works. If you look at the black and white keys on a keyboard, the whole notes (letters) are the white keys and the in-between notes are the black keys. That's about as simple as it can be.

If you look at the bass neck, and you have a full scale bass, you will see the frets along the neck. In the middle of the neck you will see dots on the third fret and then every second fret afterward. When you go down to the 13th fret, you will see a double dot. This means that there is a complete run of notes, meaning on the E string and the 12th fret is also an E, the A string on the 12th fret is also an A, and so on.

This means that there are different octaves of notes, meaning that the E notes on the bass go from the lowest note—an E and higher and higher, every subsequent E is going to be higher sounding. There are handy tricks to use the dots on the fret to make it easier to locate the notes.

Let's Get Plucking!

Today we are going to start playing the bass. We are going to start plucking the open strings, E, then A, then D, then G. But should we use a pick when we are playing or not?

Let's Ask the Titans: To Pick or Not to Pick?

I don't use a pick, I prefer finger style. That's how I started and that's what I'm used to. On some tours, I had to revert to using a pick on a couple of shows when I had blisters on my fingers from playing, but only in an emergency.

—Geezer Butler

The bass has been played with a pick on so many songs over the last sixty years that it is necessary to include that option in your arsenal of sounds, styles, and articulations.

—Shem Schroeck

I rarely play with a pick. I found it more personal to play with my fingers. There is a better connection with your fingers. All the main bass players I watched were all finger players. I heard Carol Kaye play on recordings, but that wasn't the style I gravitated towards. I associated it with guitar players that had an older style of bass playing.

—Neil Jason

I tell guitar players when they are trying to learn the bass to first learn with their fingers only. This applies even if you learn to play with a pick later—a lot of great players do.

   It's the only way to get "inside" the bass strings. It's really important to understand bass vocabulary; it's a whole language in itself. You can't understand the bass until you internalize the vocabulary of the bass through your fingers and finger techniques.

—Sean Lennon

I use both. I recently did a whole tour just playing pick with Al Di Meola.

—Armand Sabal-Lecco

I'd played for forty years with my fingers. In 2007 I injured the middle finger on my right hand, which turned into tendonitis. I realized that my career would be over unless I switched from fingers to a pick. Interestingly, Creedence's biggest hit is "Have You Ever Seen The Rain?" and I used a pick on that track. It was a challenge at first. With a pick, you get a clearer tone with more attack. I made that switch and haven't looked back.

—Stu Cook

Having previously been a guitarist, I started playing bass with a pick. I still use a pick 80 percent of the time now. I would advise beginners to use fingers if that feels good to them. But don't ignore using a pick when it feels right.

—Dave Pegg

I find playing with my fingers gives me a nicer marriage between myself and the kick drum. This is true especially with a miked kick drum that has a pointed click attack. If I play with a pick, and the kick and my note placement are not in perfect time, there can be a lot of flamming. If I play with my fingers, I can dampen the sound coming out of the speaker. I can play behind the kick and let it be the attack point. However, I do use a pick on rock recordings sometimes.

—Kenny Lee Lewis

It's helpful to know both methods. It's another tool in the toolbox that gives you a different sound. It allows you to choose what's appropriate in different situations. I started out with a pick in a high school jazz band. The first day I had to put down picks because the teacher wanted me to use my fingers too. I'm glad because I can now use both methods.

—Eva Gardner

I started playing with pick, I thought it was faster. I was also a guitar player first.

I couldn't play with my fingers. Luckily I started with a bass teacher who also played guitar. He played with his fingers, he played like he also didn't play guitar.

He told me, "You gotta learn to play with your fingers. You will eventually be able to play faster than if you used a pick." Now if I want to, I can make my fingers sound like pick and vice versa. You should learn to play with both. Like a drummer, you should play both traditional and match grip. Choosing depends on the sound and the comfortable groove.

All the Wrecking Crew studio songs from LA were made with Fenders with flat-wound strings and a pick. All the Beach Boys bass parts were made with a pick.

To contrast, all the Motown tunes were fingers. And both equally as influential.

—DANIEL MIRANDA

I use both. Some people play with a pick and you can't even tell. Steve Swallow is a Jazz bass player who uses a pick but doesn't sound like it.

—GAIL ANN DORSEY

It's whatever the song needs. I'm not a pick player, I prefer using my fingers. I can if I have to. McCartney used to play with a plectrum on the old Beatles records.

—KENNY PASSARELLI

Bass sounds bigger and more solid with your fingers. In the very early days before we became the Alice Cooper group, we were called the Spiders. We were doing eight sets per weekend and I was using my fingers. I basically wore the meat off my fingers so I had to use a pick.

I tried using Band-Aids but they wouldn't stay on. I started using a pick then. After that we started writing our own material. We were looking for our own sound and style. I started writing bass parts that were inspired by the surf song "Miserlou" by Dick Dale. You could play that with fingers but it doesn't have the percussive feel I wanted. I would go for more of a percussive sound and the growl of the pickups. The reason that you can hear every note on the original Alice Cooper records is because I avoided boomy tones that would get muddled with the floor toms. I gave up the big bottom tones for the punch.

—DENNIS DUNAWAY

I'd love to be able to do both. There is a bit of anti-pick prejudice out there.

I'm not sure why. Playing a P-Bass with a pick in a punk band is a glorious sound.

I encourage people to play with fingers too. Some people think that pick playing isn't real playing. This is despite the fact that it's been disproven a hundred times.

—MICHAEL MANRING

It's a great sound with a pick. One day I'm going to learn to use a pick properly.

There are some amazing pick players like Anthony Jackson and Bobby Vega.

—HADRIEN FERAUD

I think playing with a pick is cheating. I think you use your fingers unless it's a really fast song. Back in the eighties I was playing live with Johnny Thunders. We did this one gig in Australia. We would play one really fast song that I used a pick for in the third song in the set. I didn't know what to do with the pick when I was done with the song so I put it in between my teeth. The review of the show said, "The gig was fantastic, but it was really silly that Glen Matlock stuck his tongue out the whole time." I thought, "I didn't stick my tongue out." When I went back the next night, I got the pick out of the little pocket in my jeans. I realized that my pick was pink. So I didn't do it after that.

—GLEN MATLOCK

I am recording a Beatles track. Paul used a pick in his Beatles songs. I tried it with a pick but it wasn't soulful enough the way that I was doing it.

Anthony Jackson was amazing. He used a pick better than anybody I have ever heard.

Chris Squire was always a hero of mine and he also used a pick. I like using all of my hands and fingers to play, like palming, muting, and my thumbs.

—WYZARD

I started off as a young Victor Wooten worshipper with no pick at all. When some would equate the bass to guitar I would say "heck no, this is a bass, not a guitar!" When I moved to LA I wanted to be versatile and play more gigs. So when I was in Hanson, I would start to break out the pick for some songs. When I joined the Zappa band I had a chance to go through the original master tracks. Since I was a huge Zappa fan, this was a dream for me. I noticed that Scott Thunes and Tom Fowler always played with a pick. I then began to notice that a lot of my influences like Mike Rutherford, Chris Squire all used picks! I said "Oh my God, I've been wrong this whole time." Now I have to eat my words and go 50/50 with the pick and fingers.

—PETER GRIFFIN

Do what the music asks for and demands. Do what the song asks for. Learn as many tools, styles, and techniques as possible.

—ARIANE CAP

I think that students should start with their fingers. I've never used a pick. Most people who use a pick are ex-guitar players.

—Verdine White

A lot of bassists think that "pick" is a dirty word. For the first two years of bass playing, I used my fingers. When I joined Blue Öyster Cult, they recommended that I play with a pick. Your parts become a lot more precise when you use a pick. I am more of a pick player; it's more comfortable. I occasionally play with fingers. With a ballad you can play with fingers or thumbs. I used to think that you never mixed the two. But over the years I've seen a lot of people do both very well.

—Joe Bouchard

I learned bass through a guitar player who gave me an option of using the pick or not. I'm a nineties kid so a lot of the bass players used a pick in the grunge years. Chris Squire was another fantastic pick player. I don't get snobbish because it's just another technique. I now play with my fingers. Sometimes a pick can give you a tone that your fingers can't.

—Julie Slick

When I was younger I had the militant attitude to only play with your fingers. As I got older I realized that there are sometimes where a pick will sound better. When a heavy metal drummer does a double bass beat, it will sound even and louder if you use a pick. I still prefer fingerstyle. It's a lot nastier and not super perfect, which I love. A tiny bit of sloppiness gives it so much character.

—Mike Lepond

I use both, depending on what sound I need to get. I mainly use my fingers. I do use a pick to get a really bright sound with loads of attack and to get that Carol Kaye on Pet Sounds *feel. You also have to put foam under the bridge to get that "wooden clunk." As an aside, the older I've got the more I seem to shorten the sustain of notes. This is also a bit of a fad, at the moment. I think bass players might be playing more percussively today.*

—Mark Bedford

I love all of it. I loved Anthony Jackson's playing. I didn't realize how he was getting that sound until a guitar player picked up a bass and started using a pick on the strings. I then figured it out. I started using a pick. This came in handy when I played a certain period of the Rolling Stones music, like the sixties and seventies songs. I started using it when I played electric jazz.

—Darryl Jones

I don't feel comfortable playing with a pick. I used to be anti-pick. Now it really depends on the tune and the tone you want. If you want a clear tone, then use a pick. Even when I played guitar I never played with a pick. Your hands are the best tools you have. I don't like a pick because it's not the extension of the hand, it's another added step.

—Tony Saputo

I don't usually play with a pick. But on all the Pink Floyd stuff that I played on, I used a pick. I feel more comfortable playing with my fingers.

—Guy Pratt

I hate the sound of picks. I never could get to grips with them. They always sounded like a failed guitar player to me. I like the sound of fingers on strings. That's how a bass should sound like.

—Suzi Quatro

What Can We Glean?

Most of the experts agree that both have their place. For now we are going to try using our fingers first. If this feels really bad to you and hurts your finger too much, please feel free to use a pick. You can get picks at the guitar shop. But for this challenge, we are going to proceed with our fingers. After we have a bit of technique under our belts, then we can switch to using a pick occasionally. I'm assuming that you are right-handed; if not then you should reverse this order. If you are right-handed, then your right hand will be your plucking hand and your left will be the hand that you press down on the neck.

Just for Fun! Strange Encounters

Barry Adamson meets filmmaker David Lynch for the *Lost Highway* movie soundtrack

I was really down in the tooth because I recently had a hip replacement surgery. I was in a wheelchair and couldn't even walk. So I wanted to get my stuff back in my house to work. I haven't played bass in a while and wanted to get playing again. The day after I got home, I started playing this brassy noir tune on the bass when David Lynch calls. He told me that he is doing a film called Lost Highway. *He also told me that he recently listened to my music for ten hours straight. He then sent me a piece of the film. It was weird because the song that I was playing on when he called somehow fit perfectly—that specific piece of music! There was a great bit of synchronicity going on. I sent him that the next day and he told me it was awesome. He sent me the rest of the script and we went forward. It was really bizarre.*

—BARRY ADAMSON

Introducing the Titans: #41–49

Titan #41: Dave Larue

Dave Larue played bass with the Dixie Dregs from 1988–2017 and is featured on albums like 1992's *Bring 'Em Back Alive*.

Dave LaRue is a bassist who has performed with the Dixie Dregs since 1988 and with the Steve Morse Band since 1989. He also has worked with Joe Satriani, John Petrucci, Mike Portnoy, Derek Sherinian, and Jordan Rudess among others. Dave became a member of the supergroup Flying Colors alongside long-time bandmate Steve Morse. http://www.davelarue.com/

Titan #42: Brad Smith

Brad Smith is a founding member of Blind Melon, a band that achieved quadruple platinum status and multiple Grammy nominations. He went on to produce, engineer, and co-write songs for other artists on major labels out of his commercial studio in North Hollywood.

"I find great joy and challenge in helping people tell their story through music." Brad Smith
Photo by Kim Smith

Titan #43: Trey Gunn

Trey warms up. Photo by Eric De Bruijn

In addition to his fourteen solo recordings, Trey Gunn has worked with King Crimson, David Sylvian, Robert Fripp, Vernon Reid, Brian Eno, John Paul Jones, Steven Wilson, Azam Ali, and Puscifer. Based in Seattle, he runs a media label and coaches musicians in the creative process. http://www.treygunn.com/

Titan #44: Bruce Thomas

Bruce Thomas is best known as bass player with Elvis Costello and the Attractions. He is also a session player with Suzanne Vega, Paul McCartney, Pretenders, Madness, and many others. https://www.bruce thomas.co.uk/

Bruce back in the day.
Photo by Roberta Bayley

Titan #45: Ariane Cap

Ariane Cap (aka "Ari") is a bassist, blogger, best-selling bass book author, bass course creator, and online teaching personality. Find her popular blog at ArisBassBlog .com and hear her play at ArianeCap.com.

Ariane Cap—a bassist wearing many hats.
Photo by Aren M. of Platinum Capture

Titan #46: Guy Pratt

Guy laying back a groove. Photo by Polly Samson

Guy Pratt has played bass for everyone from Pink Floyd to Michael Jackson, Roxy Music, Whitesnake, Elton John, and countless others.

Titan #47: Jah Wobble

Jah Wobble—a man of many talents.
Photo by Alex Hurst

Jah Wobble is an English bass guitarist, singer, poet, and composer. He was the original bass player in Public Image Ltd (PIL).

Titan #48: Darryl Jones

Darryl Jones has been touring and recording with the Rolling Stones since 1993. He has also played in bands with Miles Davis and Sting.

We rehearsed in New York City in a studio next to where Sting was recording his first solo album. Darryl Jones was the bass player on that album. We rehearsed next to him for a month while we were both recording. It was amazing and also hard to keep our minds on the album because we knew Sting was right next door!

—Joe Bouchard

A live action shot of Darryl. Photo by J. Bouquet

Titan #49: Mark Stoermer

Mark Stoermer—live and in action! Photo by Rob Loud

Mark Stoermer is best known as the bassist for the Killers. He also joined Smashing Pumpkins to tour for the band's ninth studio album.

Day 5: "Future Titan of Bass" Challenge Action Step

1.   Visit http://www.bassguitarbeginner.com for Day 5 of the challenge.
2.   Visit the "Titans of Bass" Facebook group (details in "How to Use This Book" section).
3.   Visit the YouTube channel (details in "How to Use This Book" section).

String Theory, Memorize E A D G Strings, Start Plucking

So now we know to start playing with our fingers. We are going to start plucking the open strings with our fingers to get used to the feel and technique. E A D G. We are going to try to get a good sound out of it.

Practice striking the E string note once every ten seconds. Do this five times in one-minute increments: practice one minute, rest one minute, practice another minute, rest, and so on. Do these three intervals. Then do the next string A, in the same pattern, three times. Then move onto the D string, three minutes. The last is the top G string.

Get used to how the strings feel, and how alternating the use of your index and middle fingers feels and the tone you can get used to. This basic striking of long, drawn-out whole notes and letting the strings ring is the start of our journey. It's a great accomplishment to be able to strike and hold a whole note to let ring out and sound good, so it's great we are starting now.

Ɖay 6
Secret Titan Song!

Food for Thought

Learning the bass or any instrument breaks down to two areas.

1. *The first is the physical learning and playing a particular piece of the instrument. You hear something in your head and make it come out of the instrument. This is a mechanical problem; you don't yet have the capability in your fingers. Because you have limited mechanical availability in your fingers, you have to learn the mechanics of the instrument. As you remove the physical handicap of how to play the notes, you will develop and progress as a better player. The purpose of playing scales and exercises is to basically free up your fingers to not think about what your fingers are doing anymore. It gets to the point where you think of something and know how to play it. If you approach it from that angle, it's a lot less daunting than playing for no reason. If you say "Why am I doing this?"—then it's a problem. It's important to connect to the exercise, and find something useful to what you are doing. It's about answering the big why. It's important to have a particular reason to learn and exercise to make it appealing to play. It would be like if you had a map, and I put you in a dark room and told you to use that map to navigate around. It's interesting to a point, but if I gave you a map and said go find the treasure at the end of this, you would be way more motivated. You now have a goal and a location and you actually get a practical way to get out there and do it. It's much more motivating and gratifying.*

2. *The second is "What is it that you actually play?" This part is much more generic. It's about your soul and what you are hearing in your head.*

You have to learn both of these.

—Phil Soussan

So in keeping with the wisdom of our Titan Phil Soussan, we are going to give you a mission and a treasure at the end. First I'm going to share what the treasure is, and then we are going to provide a map or outline on how to achieve it. Sound cool?

The Treasure Is: Learning Your First Song on Bass!

By attempting your first song on bass, it's a real-world, awesome example that you can be proud of to show your friends and loved ones your progress. You see, you are going to play this song live to your family and friends at the end of your journey on day 14!

Keep the treasure and goal in mind and it will give you a reason to keep pushing ahead and learning the bass. The valuable lessons you learn now can help you immediately and forever in your future as a Titan of Bass! I hope you are pumped and ready to go as this is a milestone.

The Titans of Bass Song!

Following our KISS mantra, we are going to heed some more of the wisdom of the Titans.

The first thing you should do is learn to play the blues, whether you want to play them or not. When I was teaching I would tell my students to learn to play the 12-bar blues. If they didn't want to learn it, I couldn't teach them. The blues are the absolute basics, and they teach you about the foundation of music. It teaches you more about what you feel inside. There is not a lot of technique needed in the blues, yet you have time to play with heart and feeling. That's your real personality. You don't have to play like other people or everything you have learned, you can just be yourself and be more creative. When you take your blues foundation to other genres like jazz or rock, you will always have the experience of playing the blues. It's a very strong musical foundation. A lot of rock bands start off listening to the blues, like the Rolling Stones and Eric Clapton. They will always have the blues as their musical foundation.

—Russell Jackson

Learn a simple blues song.

—Bunny Brunel

A 12-bar blues song is a good place to start with bass playing and constructing basslines.

—Peter Trewavas

A bass player also needs to know how to play the 12-bar classic blues songs. This allows them to explore the bass for simple single and quarter notes with solid grooves.

—Joe Bouchard

Let's follow this advice and pick a really easy classic blues/folk song to play. I wanted to pick a three-note song with easy chord changes so you could pick up the bass and go with it as quickly as possible. I found "The Midnight Special," an ancient folky blues song that has been redone and played live by tons of artists like CCR, Paul McCartney. Even ABBA has covered it. Wow!

It's got a good groove to it, it's a blues song, and you only have to play three notes throughout! This probably won't be your favorite song; it's an exercise we want to do. The aim is to get you playing the notes and changes to create a foundation for playing other songs that you like. My suggestion is to start here, and then quickly pick a favorite song of yours to learn right afterward. Sift through the list and see if there are any songs the Titans recommended that you want to tackle soon after.

The Titan Song: "The Midnight Special"

It's in the key of C and uses three notes: F, G, and C in the same pattern. There is one bit that the chords strum out a little longer, but it's very simple. The timing changes, but the notes don't. There is a lot of pausing and mostly whole notes being played.

So when we play it, you will learn three chord changes, three places to put your fingers on the fretboard. It allows us to start playing something that you can show your friends and family that they will recognize and probably have heard before or at least know about. So it's a win-win and great song to start on!

Introducing the Titans: #50–57

Titan #50: Kenny Lee Lewis

Kenny playing on Steve Miller hit—"Jet Airliner."
Photo by Kim Smith Miller

California native Kenny Lee Lewis grew up influenced by the San Francisco Bay
Area sound of the 1960s and 1970s being broadcast by Pirate FM radio station
WSAN up the Delta in his hometown of Sacramento. After playing in local
bands and college jazz orchestras, he moved to Los Angeles in 1973 and became
a studio musician, singer, writer, and eventually joined up with the Steve Miller
Band in 1982. He has been with the band both as guitarist and bassist for over
thirty-eight years. www.kennyleelewis.com; www.stevemillerband.com

Titan #51: Liam Wilson

Liam Wilson is best known for being the bass player for the Dillinger Escape Plan and many other projects, namely Azusa and John Frum. You can follow him on Twitter @liam wilson, Instagram @Liam_Wilson, and Facebook @liamwilsonbass.

Liam tearing it up.
Photo by Rob Wallace

Titan #52: Bjorn Englen

Bjorn screaming for the bass!
Photo by Lars Andersson

Upon arrival to the United States, the Swedish-born virtuoso bassist quickly became known as the bass player for multiplatinum Quiet Riot from 1994–1995. As a versatile session bassist he has recorded on well over fifty albums of various genres, and performed nearly 2,000 live shows.

Titan #53: Colin Edwin

Colin Edwin—live and on the scene. Photo by Caroline Traitler

Colin Edwin was a member of the British progressive rock band Porcupine Tree.
www.colinedwin.co.uk

Music can open doors like nothing else can, and the bass has been my key to go where I never imagined possible.

—COLIN EDWIN

Titan #54: Kenny Passarelli

Kenny played bass on the 1975 Elton John
album *Rock of the Westies.*

Kenny Passarelli is one of the first bassists to use a fretless bass and is well known for his time with Elton John in the mid-seventies. https://en.wikipedia.org/wiki/Kenny_Passarelli

Titan #55: Scott Thunes

Scott Thunes with his vintage Fender. Photo by Scott Thunes

Scott Thunes is a bassist, bass synth player, and backing vocalist, and was rehearsal director with Frank Zappa as a member of the official Zappa Band from 1981–1988. He is a teaching artist in the Rock Band program at Marin School of the Arts, Novato, California.

I love his playing—it's similar to the way he talks in a confident, intelligent genius-composer sort of way. I was such a huge fan when I joined the Zappa Band. It was crazy taking his place on the bass and trying to play the bass parts.

—Peter Griffin

Scott was unique with his classic conservatory background mixed with his punk attitude. When you took his very unusual influences and applied them to the Frank Zappa repository, something really magical happened. He came from a completely different angle than most bass players.

—Bryan Beller

Titan #56: Derek Frank

Derek Frank: LA session player. Photo by Myriam Santos

Derek Frank is a touring/session bass player living in Los Angeles. Currently, he is a member of both Gwen Stefani's and Shania Twain's bands, and has released two albums as a leader.

Titan #57: Jon Button

Jon Button is a bassist living in Los Angeles known for his work with The Who, Sheryl Crow, Shakira, Robben Ford, and many others.

Jon Button at your service.
Photo by Cameron Jordan

Day 6: "Future Titan of Bass" Challenge Action Step

1. Visit http://www.bassguitarbeginner.com for Day 6 of the challenge.
2. Visit the "Titans of Bass" Facebook group (details in "How to Use This Book" section).
3. Visit the YouTube channel (details in "How to Use This Book" section).

The Titans of Bass special song! Listen to different versions of the song. Listen to the song without the bass notes. Keep on plucking.

Now that we know what our Titan song is, "The Midnight Special," google it and listen to the different versions and interpretations of it. As there are supposed to be hundreds of versions of it around, listen to the melody, structure, and how the song goes.

This song is great because you can play, record, and redo it as much as you want because no one owns the original recordings. In fact, no one really knows who actually wrote the original!

After listening to a few versions, now it's time to check out the version we are looking at. We are going to listen to the version of the bass today. In fact, it's just guitar and singing.

Listen to the parts of the song; there is an introduction, then the verses. The song structure stays the same.

As you can tell, the song is a little fast. This song is a great one to learn on as you can play the bass simply and then make it jazzier if you wish. Today your assignment is to listen to the song a couple times. The only time it changes a lot is at the beginning and the ending. Listen to the structure and the guitar chords. This version has the bass to copy. I have made it as simple as it can be while still making the song complete.

Today we are going to repeat the open string plucking exercise. To summarize: Practice plucking each of the four open strings (EADG) once every ten seconds. Practice in one-minute intervals. Again, get use to the "feel" of striking the strings with your index and middle fingers. Really try to "hear" the notes being drawn out.

Tip: Download the version of "1: The Midnight Special—Bass Track" from the titan website http://www.bassguitarbeginner.com/. Look for the link for today's lesson from the YouTube channel. Download to your iPhone/phone tablet.

Start listening to the song with the bass track five times with your headphones every day. It should take about fifteen minutes total. This is an easy way for your mind to grasp what's happening so that you really get used to it.

Day 7

Connect-the-Dots Adventure

Play Note #1: C

How are you feeling about your journey so far? You have come a long way. You now own a bass and an amp, you know how to tune, you have practice plucking the strings, and you even have your "first song" to learn to play live at the end of your journey.

Now it comes down to learning a bit about music to get started. As you know, my mission of this challenge/journey is to get you as the readers a chance to give the bass a try.

Instead of providing complicated groove tabs, I wanted to simplify the act of learning as a "jumping off" point to get you started on your journey. So we are going to learn a simple way to figure out how the bass is organized through notes and keys.

Connect-the-Dots Adventure

Do you like video games? I do. I'm so ancient I love all the old Super Mario NES 8-bit games. Now it's awesome because you can play them with an online emulator. Think about what you are really doing in a video game. I know you are saving the princess or shooting aliens or banking points, but what are you really doing? Pushing buttons, right? It doesn't sound that hard, or interesting, but that's what it is.

Playing music and the bass guitar is sort of the same concept. You are just playing notes. Like games, the combination of the right buttons at the right time means you win. But it's even better with the bass. Instead of some games, like *Street Fighter II*, where you sometimes have to press three or more buttons and arrows at the same time, 99 percent of the time with bass, it's one note at a time. The most intensive action on the bass would be "holding" a note, like you would "hold a button."

Take a look at the bass and hold it in your lap. Look at the dots. These dots are there to create visual clues on what notes "or buttons" to play. So if you can remember some patterns from your favorite games (and I'm sure you can), you can learn some basic bass patterns. So think of it kind of like a "Connect-the-Dots Adventure"! You can think of it like the "Guitar Hero" or "Rock Band" video game series too—those are so much fun!

This might take a few days to learn completely, but the rewards are amazing! If you understand this, you will have an amazing way to learn and process notes. This matters because if you know the "key" notes, you know the "right notes" to play in a song. It's a big deal!

So to explain this Connect-the-Dots Adventure, I'd now like to introduce bass titan Rev Jones.

Introducing the Titans: #58

Titan #58: Rev Jones

Rev Jones has seen a lot of stage time. Photo by Brian K. Denton BKD Photo

Known for his distinctive two-handed tapping style and over-the-neck fingering technique, Rev Jones has recorded and toured with Steelheart, Leslie West/ Mountain, Michael Schenker, Fuel, Paul Gilbert, George Thorogood, George Lynch, and many others. http://www.revjones.com

When I started playing, I took lessons with this teacher named Jim Miller.

1. *He started off showing me how a scale was made up. A scale had seven notes that make up a key. The seven notes are: A B C D E F G*

2. *For example, we started with the key of G: G A B C D E F#.*

3. *He then got me to grab a piece of paper and draw a picture of the four strings on the bass neck: (E A D G) and the frets.*

4. *Then I was to take the seven notes (G A B C D E F#) and split them up, and draw them on the frets using circles. The rules were to draw in three of the notes per string. I put Xs on the strings, three per string with seven notes. So I took the seven notes and put Xs on their locations on the strings.*

5. *My teacher said, "Just split it up into three notes per string. There are all your patterns. Follow the same patterns down the string, they are all the same."*

When I learned this, it took me only two months to realize most music theory. I saw how everything works mathematically.

If you are new to music, you will get this simple concept even quicker. There are no major/minor keys or modes. There are only seven notes! It would be better if there weren't names for the notes but numbers. After I wrote it out, I put my bass on my lap and I could see how the patterns looked both backwards and forwards.

—Rev Jones

Thanks, Rev!

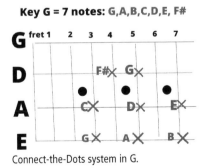

Connect-the-Dots system in G.

Our End Goal

So the end goal is to take the seven notes in a key and write them down as three notes per string. This will help us learn the patterns or the "right notes" to play in every song. All you need to know is the key of the song and you can play it!

I know right now this might be a bit to process, but I'd ask that you be patient with this because of how powerful it is to learn this. By writing out this exercise and starting with a blank piece of paper, it allows your mind to visualize and imagine the fretboard. After you understand where the "seven buttons" are, you will be surprised at how quickly you progress. Pretty cool, hey?

Now It's Your Turn!

Here's what you need:

Paper (a notebook is good)
Pen/pencil—a marker is great
A ruler (optional but awesome to have)
Your bass
A few minutes

You saw how the notes in the key of G were mapped out with the drawing. Now we are going to learn about the key of C. This is the key that our "Midnight Special" song is in. The pitches or notes of C major are C, D, E, F, G, A, and B. So we are going to take these notes and draw them on our bass picture or map. It's like connecting the dots. Follow along with the steps:

1. Draw four horizontal lines across the page like so:

Draw out step 1.

2. As you know, the four open strings are G, D, A, and E. The E string would be at the bottom of your bass when you hold it; it's the largest string. Label each string on the left side like so:

Draw out step 2.

3. Now let's draw the vertical lines in, which are the frets of our bass. Draw seven vertical lines evenly across the page from left to right that represent our frets.

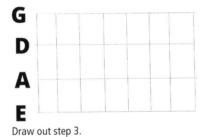

Draw out step 3.

4. To make it easier, we are going to label the frets at the top from 1 to 7. This doesn't officially represent anything; it will just help us to draw the bass as we see it.

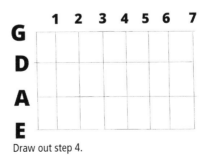

Draw out step 4.

5. Now let's scribe in some circles to make it easy to find the notes we need. Draw three circles in the middle of the strings at frets between 2 and 3, 4 and 5, and 6 and 7. The dots belong in between the D and A string. Look at your bass and you should see them.

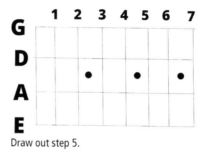

Draw out step 5.

6. So that's the basic design of the bass from frets 1 to 7. Now the game begins! We are going to draw out the seven notes of the C major scale in three notes per string. The seven notes to use are C, D, E, F, G, A, and B. We will go one by one. Please follow along. Let's start with the C note. Mark an X on the first note on the correct place like in the picture. It's on the A string, third fret right next to the dot.

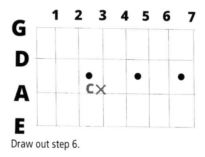

Draw out step 6.

7. The next note is D. Go to the right on the A string to the next dot, the fifth fret, and mark it down.

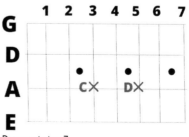

Draw out step 7.

8. Mark the third E note. It's on the seventh fret, A string by the third dot.

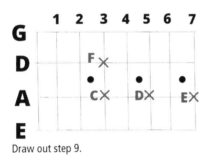

Draw out step 8.

9. Our first string is done, we have three notes on one string. Look at your bass. If you want, carefully put the bass on the ground with the E string on the bottom. Check out the notes we wrote down for a moment. It's on the seventh fret, A string by the third dot. Move on to the fourth note, F, on the D string, third fret, right above the C note.

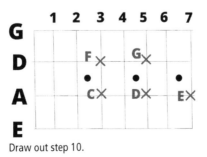

Draw out step 9.

10. Mark the fifth G note. It's on the fifth fret, D string by the second dot.

Draw out step 10.

11. Mark the sixth A note. It's on the seventh fret, D string by the third dot.

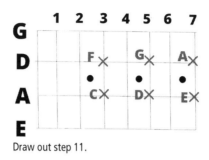

Draw out step 11.

12. Last note—now we move to the top G string fourth fret and mark down the B note.

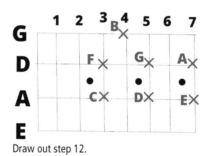

Draw out step 12.

There we go, all seven notes for the C key. As "Midnight Special" is in the key of C, we only need to use the F, C, and D notes in the song.

Why Is It Great to Start with the Key of C?

C major was the most popular key after a study was conducted on 1,300 of the most popular songs in the last five decades. In fact, 26 percent of the most popular songs were in the key of C! So by learning the C key and "The Midnight Special" very well, you will have a head start to learning many of these popular songs.

The Key: A Good Place to Start and Finish

Most of the time, the song will begin and end with the same note as the key that it's in. To simplify, you can safely assume that most songs in the key of C will both start and end with a C note. This is probably true 95 percent of the time. This is how you see musicians play a song on the spot from just knowing what key it is in. The key is both our starting point and ending point.

It's pretty easy to "connect the dots" after we know where they are visually. Use the dots as pattern guides to know what the right notes to play are.

The seven notes in the key are the "seven buttons" to press. Master the right buttons in the right song, and you will nail it! In our Titan song "The Midnight Special" we only need to know and play three notes in the C scale—F, C, and G. So for now, just stick to and learn these—think of them like the right "buttons" to the song. Awesome, you are doing so well!

Let's Ask the Titans: What Age Did You Start Playing the Bass?

The earliest memory I have is of starting to play at the age of two. I'm the youngest of five musician brothers—when I was born, they needed a bass player and that became me.

—Victor Wooten

When I was twelve years old my dad got a hold of a Fender Mustang bass for my brother to play, seeing that all the men in my household played the drums, myself included. He didn't play it that much, but I used to pick it up and play it all the time just for fun, and it seemed to come very natural to me.

—Shem Schroeck

I started playing bass really late. Back in the day, I went over to a friend's house.

He had this bass with only two strings on it. He told me I could have it, so I started to play it.

The weekend after, I was out buying the other two strings to complete the set. I saw this advertisement from Howard Devoto in a magazine. They were looking for musicians for their band. I had only been playing for three or four days, yet I answered the advertisement and got the gig! That's punk rock for you.

—Barry Adamson

I started playing bass when I was nineteen, when I joined what would become Black Sabbath. I originally played rhythm guitar, inspired by my favorite band, the Beatles.

—GEEZER BUTLER

I was fourteen when I started playing the bass. I got money from newspaper sales. I saved up and went to a guitar shop in Long Island and bought a bass. It was the best musical move I ever made.

—JEFF BERLIN

I started writing songs at the age of thirteen or fourteen. I've never played the bass on a stage but I play it constantly when I'm writing and when I'm recording.

—JOAN ARMATRADING

I was fifteen when I picked the bass up. I'd taken piano since the age of seven and cello since ten, but when I saw my older brother play bass with his band and people at the show having a blast I was like, "Hold it! THAT IS WHAT I WANNA DO!" And I did.

—MARY HUFF

At fifteen. I bought a Rosetti Bass 8 from a kid at school. It cost me £6. I didn't know how to play it but then moved to a homemade Fender Mustang–like bass, which was the instrument I played my first performances on.

—HORACE PANTER

My big brother listened to a lot of progressive rock. I ended up loving a lot of complicated music like Genesis and Gentle Giant. It all changed when I was sixteen. I heard the Sex Pistols and all the progressive stuff was done for me. It was motivating because I could actually play like they did. I loved punk rock because it was about getting started, being in a band, and getting girls.

—BILLY GOULD

I had gone along to audition for The Uglys as a guitarist, but my friend Roger Hill, who was much better than me, got the gig. However, their bassist was leaving and the vocalist, Steve Gibbons, offered me the job as bassist. I bought John's '62 Precision Bass off him for £80 and became a bass player. It really changed my life.

—DAVE PEGG

I was very fortunate with Public Image because I was a complete beginner. In '77 I was only playing for a year, teaching myself in a squat—I didn't have an amp. I leaned a high-action bass against the headboard. All the other furniture had been burnt and taken away—all that was left was the headboard not even the bed. I had to lean it against that to get a sound. It's like all these old blues players that would be a string against a door-frame and pluck it. You develop a good sound, a good feeling with your fingers. In 1978, less that year later living in the squat, I was with PIL with a nice, shiny precision bass. I was able to play by my own rules when learning these basslines. I wasn't like so many bass players coming into bands with a dominant guitarist who says, "Play these chords." They liked what I did so I was able to create basslines. I couldn't even count at that time—you couldn't even count me in. I have a natural sense of timing. There are so many young musicians who are criticized that some end up losing enthusiasm. Their natural talent doesn't happen. I was lucky.

—Jah Wobble

Just for Fun! Don't Try This at Home!

Zany Zappa zingers: Scott Thunes flips for Frank

We played in an Austrian city back in the day. We started off playing "Dancin' Fool." The song starts up with this fanfare riff, guitar and piano clunking away. During this part, I climbed on the risers and jumped off the stage. I landed on the ground. I landed so close to Frank that he forgot the words to the song. He stood there looking with the microphone, looking blank.

Frank used to love it when other people messed up because he could say, "That's inexcusable. Let's start from the top." In this case, I didn't mess up my playing, but I made him forget the words. When this happens, there's a couple ways to fix it. The band can keep on playing the song. The song would cycle through until the singer started again at the next four bars. Almost no one would have noticed this. But instead of this choice, he ended up completely stopping the band. Instead of yelling at me, he said, "Mr. Thunes, get back on the riser and do it again," as if somehow he'd messed up, and admitted that he forgot the words. I still think about it all the time.

—Scott Thunes

Just for Fun: "Oh my Godzilla!"

Thirty years and thirty-five movies in, Blue Öyster Cult hit paydirt with 2019's *Godzilla: King of the Monsters* movie.

Blue Öyster Cult's "Godzilla" was a great song when we released it in 1977. It's also one of the most fun songs to play live. They have made over thirty Godzilla movies over the years. For all those years, whenever we heard there was going to be a new Godzilla movie released, our publishing company and the band would try to get the movie producers to use our song in it. They never did until over thirty years later in 2019's Godzilla: King of the Monsters, *the thirty-fifth movie in the Godzilla franchise. It was great because in the end credits, our song "Godzilla" appears. The way we recorded our song used a little dry humor.*

—Joe Bouchard

Introducing the Titans: #59–67

Titan #59: Julie Slick

Julie plays bass on the Echotest album
Daughter of Ocean.

Julie Slick is a virtuoso bassist and composer known for her wide array of unique tones and substantial melodic invention. https://julieslick.com/

Titan #60: Barry Adamson

Barry Adamson was Magazine's and Nick Cave and the Bad Seeds' basso profundo. He has also performed on numerous studio albums, released a solo album, and continues to be in demand, touring globally. https://www.lexermusic.com/barry-adamson

Barry Adamson: Punk Rock original.
Photo by Joné Reed

Titan #61: Tonina Saputo

Tonina and her double bass. Photo by Jessica J. Page

Tonina is a bassist, vocalist, and composer from St. Louis, Missouri. @iamtonina

Titan #62: Dennis Dunaway

Dennis playing live with Alice Cooper.
Photo by Phillip Solomonson

Dennis Dunaway is best known as the original bass guitarist for the rock band Alice Cooper. The band was inducted into the Rock & Roll Hall of Fame in 2011. Dennis co-wrote some of the band's most notable songs, including "School's Out," which was inducted into the Grammy Hall of Fame in 2015. www.dennisdunaway.com

I've been working with Dennis many years, after the original Alice Cooper band dissolved and I got out of the Blue Öyster Cult. I wanted to be a guitar player so Dennis was the bass player in our Blue Coupe band. He is talented, fantastic, creative, and has a good stage presence. I learned a lot watching him play in the original Alice Cooper band. We opened for them back in 1971.

—Joe Bouchard

Titan #63: Klaus Flouride

Klaus and his special bass. Photo by Andrew Ramone–Andrea Bertocchi

Klaus is a founding member of the Dead Kennedys. He plays a custom-made Schroom bass, and he collects 78 rpm records and 1960s budget guitars.

Titan #64: Chuck Dukowski

Chuck Dukowski is a punk rock bassist, songwriter, and founding member of Black Flag.

A bass player that influenced me a lot subconsciously was Chuck Dukowski.

It was his insane execution, the wild madman that he was onstage with Black Flag.

It was very inspiring. It was like how Keith Moon's or Ginger Baker's wild playing style inspired drummers. They were explosive live.

—Harley Flanagan

Chuck rocking out in Riot Fest Denver.
Photo by Chris Shary

Titan #65: Glen Matlock

Glen lays it down live; Glen Matlock and his band the Philistines 2010 album *Born Running*.

From the Sex Pistols, Rich Kids, Iggy Pop, and with a whole lot in between, to the Faces—Glen says, "Now I got my own thing going on." www.glenmatlock.co.uk/

—Glen Matlock

Titan #66: Gerald Casale

Gerald rocking it with Devo.
Photo by Michael Pilmer

Devo founder and co-principal songwriter, including "Whip It," "Freedom of Choice," and "Beautiful World," Gerald Casale is also an award-winning music video and commercial director.

At one point in the seventies, I was telling everybody that "rock was dead." Then Devo came out and blew everything out of the water for me. Not only is Gerald Casale an amazing bass player, he's also an amazing songwriter. He understands rock and roll. This lets him add different things into their music to make it sound good.

—Scott Thunes

Titan #67: Mary Huff

Mary Huff and her bass.
Photo by Muncy Fine Photography

For over thirty years, bassist Mary Huff has been entertaining crowds worldwide, serving up a greasy mix of country-fried garage rock, surf, R&B, and rockabilly with her band Southern Culture On The Skids. Mary's bass playing has been showcased in numerous movies and TV shows and has been featured in *Vintage Guitar* and *Bass Guitar* magazines.

Day 7: "Future Titan of Bass" Challenge Action Step

1. Visit http://www.bassguitarbeginner.com for Day 7 of the challenge.
2. Visit the "Titans of Bass" Facebook group (details in "How to Use This Book" section).
3. Visit the YouTube channel (details in "How to Use This Book" section).

Connect-the-Dots Adventure: Play Note #1: C

Listen to the song without the bass notes. Play C to get going. *Today's lesson will go over the writing of the Connect-the-Dots system—demonstration. If you haven't drawn out the Connect-the-Dots Adventure yet, watch the YouTube video to go over it and do it now.

Now that we have the KEY, let's use it as a map to see the three notes we are going to use on "The Midnight Special" song. As the key is in C, that means that normally it starts and ends with the C note. The intro starts with C and is the trickiest part of the song. One way to keep track of the song is to listen to the guitar and the words. Listen to the song three times today. We are going to learn the note that the song is in the key of, the C note.

Go to the second string, the A string, and the third note, the first circle. Look at the map you drew out to use it as a guide. Use the index finger of your left hand to press down on the fret until you get a clean noise and strum the string with your right hand. Practice playing that one note, playing it over and over in ten-note intervals. Practice this in five-minute intervals, playing that note every three seconds. Congratulations you are playing the bass!

Tip: If you haven't yet, download the version of "1: The Midnight Special—Bass Track" from the titan website http://www.bassguitarbeginner.com/ and look for the link to today's lesson on the YouTube channel. Download to your iPhone/phone tablet.

Listen to the song with the bass track five times with your headphones every day. It should take about fifteen minutes total. This is an easy way for your mind to grasp what's happening so that you really get used to it.

DAY 8
Tone and Groove
Play Note #2: F and Note #3: G

Through my journey in interviewing all of these Titans, a lot of times we ended up talking about tone and groove and what they mean to bass players. What exactly are tone and groove? And why should you pay attention? This information will be quite valuable a little later on in your bass journey.

Tone: What Is Tone and How Important Is It?

I sometimes give talks about bass. I came up with what I call "The 3 Ts of Bass Playing." They are fundamentally important. They are:

1. *Tone: You need to have a rich, warm, beautiful bass tone. Remember, it's a bass, not a treble!*
2. *Time: You need impeccable timing, without dragging or rushing.*
3. *Taste: You need to know how to play the right thing at the right time, especially during improvisation.*

If you don't have these "3 Ts" under control, you are screwed.

—ARTHUR BARROW

My concern was to play the song and perform it. There's a difference between the two. I tried to play notes to perform the song. Tone kind of happened for me. My goal was to perform.

—BILLY SHEEHAN

It's important to find a tone that inspires your playing. I like a slightly distorted tone when playing heavy stuff. I find it helps my playing.

—GEEZER BUTLER

The best players vary their tone a lot. A lot of bass players just thump along and don't give enough attention to their tone. A lot of bass players and producers prefer the bass tone to be more like a stand-up bass thumpy sound. Many match the tone of the right hand of the bass to the drummer's right foot, the kick drum. It becomes hampered tonally. They don't take advantage of higher frequencies that they could get from the electric bass. I like to split the difference with my tone. If you hear the live recording of me playing bass with Bob Dylan on the Rolling Thunder Revue, my bass has an almost guitar-like tone. On my playing on "American Pie" with Don McLean, I am playing with a pick and flat-wound strings. It has a lot of high-end sound, not too bassy. I like to blend my tone with just enough of the lower frequencies to make it percussive. I include enough of the higher frequencies so you can also hear the right-hand attack. In this way, the bass really jumps out. It is called a bass "guitar" after all. You get the best of both worlds.

—Rob Stoner

I didn't know much about it when I started. Over the years, it became more natural. With the Killers, I didn't think about it too much. It's the last element on the sound of the recording. It can make a huge difference for the listeners' experience. Even if you don't have the best gear, a huge part of the tone comes from the hands and instrument first.

—Mark Stoermer

Tone is everything—you start with the tone. Tone is the seductive mistress of the bass.

That tone will pull you in more than notes. I tell my students to start with one note when they start to play, and to find the right tone before they rip up and down the neck. Tone comes from your fingertips, your approach, your right and left hands. It's important to develop this first. Tone is when you create the atmosphere and the notes in the piece that you are working on. You need to start on that primal sublevel of you and the instrument. I think every good musician creates their signature sound. I used to park myself in front of the double bass when Charles Mingus came through in the early jazz clubs and listen to the tone he got out of it.

—Jack Casady

I firmly believe that 90 percent of your sound comes from the player himself, not the equipment. It's our hands and how we control the bass notes by using our ears. Playing with a nice even middle range can be more dynamic, not as loud as possible all the time. Consistency is a big part of it; chops come later.

—DAVE LARUE

You want to get the bass to sit right in the mix when you are live or in the studio. I work on my tone constantly. Your right hand is where the tone comes from. It's my goal to always try to get the tone possible from your hand first and your amps second.

—DEREK FRANK

While I'm playing with Uriah Heep, it's my goal to make the bass and drums sound like one instrument.

—DAVEY RIMMER

Tone is extremely important. I do a lot of mixing work for others. Sometimes I'll listen to a track and the bass playing is great but the tone is bad. I have to polish it a lot. Tone is as important as your technique and notes.

—JAMES COOK

Tone is something I've been wrestling with for forty years, every time I record. It's important for people to find a sound that rings true for them. It's about finding the right tone for each project. It doesn't always work for me to take the sound of one tone from one project to another. I'm always tweaking it every time from project to project.

—TREY GUNN

My tone has always been my bread and butter. Over the years I have seen so many good players. But they didn't understand that they would be even better players with better tone. Back when I started playing in Chicago, I wasn't very good. But I did have a good tone which got me a lot of gigs and sessions. This helped me until I learned to play a lot better. I grew up listening to James Jamerson who had a great tone. I think it's something that has to be in you. You can have all the gear and gadgets, but if you don't know how to use your fingers to develop your tone, you will always be cheating yourself. It's true that you can get a lot of great tones from gadgets. When Parliament-Funkadelic was out, I was a huge fan of Bootsy Collins and his playing. I started using some of the gear he used and started experimenting. But when I got the gig with BB King in 1979, he told me to leave all the effects at home. He said, "Just bring me ten fingers and your heart." My tone was always there, I just needed to find it again.

I haven't even used any effects since then. When you play with BB you have to play with dynamics. You had to go from being a ten to a one, but you still had to have the tone presence and intensity. I learned to use my fingers a long time ago.

—Russell Jackson

Tone is part of your vocabulary; your technique is very important. First you can play in your mind then you can physically play it. Tone is equally expressive in all instruments, not just the bass.

—Percy Jones

Tone is subjective. It has to do with the people playing with you and the kind of music you are trying to make. Your tone has to fill a space in music that's playing. You will know the right tone when you hear it. It's architectural. It's about balance and volume—the volume of the frequency range, not the sound volume.

—Gerald Casale

The most important thing is to always learn all the musical theory and proper techniques with your instrument. If you play your bass and amp and your tone is good, you will play better. But if your tone is weak, either too trebly, too bassy, it's a bummer. You will play much better if you love your sound and tone. It can give you tremendous confidence and the gig will be more fun.

—Mike Lepond

A main part of playing the bass is understanding the role of weight and the low end. This involves more feeling instead of hearing, working with the drums to create this feel. I'm not sure if you need to focus on tone but more on the feeling. But if the tone is wrong, then the feel is going to be wrong too.

—Mick Harvey

Sound is everything. Having a beautiful sound is important like time, feel, and a strong groove. Whit Browne, who taught at the Berklee College of Music, used to say "They hear you before they hear you." The main things that I help my students with are their rhythm and sound. Perfecting your sound is crucial for a recording bass player. A lot of times people call you for gigs because they dig your sound.

—JOHN PATITUCCI

I have known amazing players that are better than me, but have horrible tones. I end up having no interest in them; I usually write off the band because of it. On the other hand, I have known bad players who have amazing tones that I'm actually interested in. I try to seek pleasure in my tone. I think it's a great way to go to find the thing that makes you happy.

—BILLY GOULD

Tone is a shade or color for a musical painting. It has to complement the subject matter of the song. I think tone comes first from the players fingers, not just the instrument or the amp.

—LEO LYONS

A good bass player automatically takes care of their tone. You want to distinguish the bass from the rest of instruments in the track, yet you also want it to fit in. The bass should be an instrument to accompany others. I like a good bottom-sound with a midrange tone so you can hear what I'm doing.

—JEAN MILLINGTON

The tone and the groove tells you what genre and style you are playing in. It goes hand in hand with your playing.

—KEVIN KEITH

Whatever instrument you play, the first thing you are going to develop is your sound.

Even at home when you are practicing, you want to be able to get a good sound out of your instrument at a very low volume. I'm a firm believer in low volume playing, this way you know you are getting a full sound. Good gear helps but you want to make sure you are putting out the best sound you can with your instrument without the best gear.

—CHRISTIAN MCBRIDE

Wow, there is sure a lot of support from the Titans for making sure that you achieve a good tone or sound from your instrument. That's why it's good to go over this info now, as we are learning "The Midnight Special" Titan Song. It's a great exercise to see how we can change the feel or sound of the song by playing the notes differently. The purpose isn't to overwhelm you, it's just helpful advice that how you play the notes is more important than being the fastest or flashiest player.

Along with tone, the word groove is used a lot when we talk about the bass and drums, the rhythm section of music. So what is groove, and does it matter like tone does?

What Is "Groove" and How Important Is It?

I teach a lesson that's nicknamed "2 through 10" where I list the ten parts of music.

Notes	*Dynamics*
Rhythm	*Listening*
Tone	*Space*
Phrasing	*Technique*
Articulation	*Feel*

Groove is basically the culmination of all these parts of music working together. If any one of those is too far off, it won't groove. You could have perfect rhythm, good tone, play all the right notes, but if you are too loud, then it's not going to groove. The groove is synonymous with the "zone" in sports.

—Victor Wooten

Groove is a matter of people being in sync. Even if it's a jarring, non-rhythm[ic], inconsistent rhythm track, that could be a groove. The old progressive giants like Genesis or King Crimson had a great groove, even with odd time signatures. It depends more on an agreement than any particular definition.

—Billy Sheehan

For me, the groove is the mother. It is the one who gives us the tempo to the music and the breath to the music.

—Manou Gallo

Groove is like the pulse of life to me. It can be slow and relaxed when the mind and heart are calm and steady. It can also be fast and frantic, full of excitement and expectation. It's always measured. It's a repetition that reveals its form and feel.

—JUSTIN CHANCELLOR

Groove is something that makes people move and react emotionally to the vibration of notes and rhythms. It has to affect people in some way.

—LEO LYONS

Groove is like a fart in the wind. It's pretty elusive. You know it's there but you sure can't see it. It's almost biological and physiological. I've worked with the best drummers in the world. Yet when you sit down to play, it's different every time! Sometimes the only way to see it is to look at people's heads and feet when you are playing. If they are moving with you, then you are in the groove.

—LEE SKLAR

The rhythm and feeling are the most important part of the groove; the notes are secondary. Groove is defined by the way music makes you feel, the way the notes are put together to make you feel something.

—JAMES COOK

When the bass and drums are locked in, the guitar player has a perfect little bed to play over. Sometimes the bass has to take different roles. It can lay in the back or it can be a melodic instrument that leads the melody and a certain groove of the song. You should know how to master both roles.

—MIKE LEPOND

Bass is the main instrument in South African culture. People don't care about the guitar or piano, they care about the bass, drums, and singing. And if the bass player isn't good, they won't dance. And if they don't dance, there's a problem. So you can't be all over the place when you play.

—BAKITHI KUMALO

Why would you define it? Groove is something you feel. It's like defining love—you will know it when you feel it.

—CHRISTINA MCBRIDE

Nick Cave and the Bad Seeds' most popular song "Red Right Hand" (as featured on the
Dumb and Dumber *soundtrack) was created when I was playing bass on a jam session.*
There is a lot going on in the song from the organ riff, jazzy drum brushes, and the bell.
But the whole undertone of that song is generated by the bassline as it was first written on
the bass. Most people, after hearing the song, wouldn't realize the role of this bass in the
song. The feel and groove is created by the bass.

—MICK HARVEY

If you start analyzing it, you've already lost it. It's harder to define groove when it's not
there. I read a famous producer's book where he relates, "If the bass is milliseconds ahead
of the bass drum and the snake drum is milliseconds out, then you have a great groove."
I don't see it that way. It's not mathematical or formulaic but something indefinable. It's
like good cooking in a way. You could have all the right ingredients but the dish could be
rubbish. It's part of the magic.

—COLIN EDWIN

It's funny how they list the order of credits or credentials on albums or a concert program.
The pecking order is the drummer on bottom, then the bass, then the guitar, piano, sax-
ophone, trumpet. The singer is on the top. Groove really starts with the drums and bass
at the bottom of the foundation of the rhythm section. If they are solid, the rest of the
instruments have something to build a groove on. When the rhythm section has a swing or
pocket going, if the rest of the band is competent, they will fall in line and create a groove.
The entire song ensemble becomes locked into the same rhythmic pulse.

—ROB STONER

When you are playing with a band and you all catch a wave, you all play on the same
wavelength. You can't go wrong when you listen to all nuances and hit all the right places.
It's when you play and people have to move. That happened to us a lot when we were
playing live in Fanny. When you really hit a groove, the people move.

—JEAN MILLINGTON

It's kind of like, "What's it like being in love?" You will know it when it's there, and you
will know it when it's not there.

—ANGELINE SARIS

It's an emotional thing. It's the thing that makes you do something crazy. It moves you.

It's so funny that you have to learn all these things with amps, techniques, and how to play your instruments. But you don't have to remember the first time you went into a concert. When the band first comes out and the kick drum hits you for the first time, it makes a huge impression. Groove is all about preserving that emotion as a player. It's when you lock in with a really aggressive and good drummer. You become so tight that people can't tell if you are two instruments or one.

—KEVIN KEITH

A good groove is addictive and repetitive. It won't get monotonous, within reason. It won't deviate. There is something about the right rhythm and choice of notes. The listener attaches himself to it and they can't get enough of it.

—PERCY JONES

I don't define it. I enjoyed the groove even before I started playing bass. It's a very important part of making music meaningful and a universal way to reach people. In a way it's like a mantra or a mediation. It gains power over you as you play it over and over again. It's both a destination and a spiritual path. If you play with feeling and pocket, then you give yourself a great advantage as a bass player or drummer. It's difficult to be a really good bass player without a foundation.

—DARRYL JONES

Groove is the ability of being comfortable with yourself. It reminds me of a man who is comfortable in meditation. He is not sloppy but relaxed. A groove is relaxed—it's not trying too hard. It's like enlightenment or a stage of nonduality. It's like looking at the pictures of food but not tasting it. It's like describing the taste of cinnamon exactly. You just can't. You are in time, because you are in time—you are adroit of time. A bit of it is a variation or an improvised thing. It's like you lost yourself but came back around. Then you think, "we were in a concert?" You went somewhere else. When you look at time, it breaks down to a: second, half-second, millisecond. There really isn't the smallest measure of time. Time does not exist, probably. It's an indivisible thing; it's empty. I don't really exist right now. I'm a compound of things. Musicians are often ahead of the curve on spiritual stuff. Music is formless—it's hard to impose grammars on it, but we try. Everything is all phenomena and impermanence. If we try to cling to last night's groove, we can't. We can't be in yesterday's groove, but some musicians try to hang on to the coattails of their past.

—Jah Wobble

So there you have it, we can see that tone and groove are an important aspect of learning and playing the bass. Mull over this information and think about what it means to us learning how to play our song in the challenge.

Introducing the Titans: #68–76

Titan #68: Ben Ellis

Ben Ellis live. Photo by Paul McAlpine

Ben Ellis is a live sound engineer and bassist located in London, United Kingdom, who currently plays bass with Iggy Pop, Razorlight, and Swervedriver.

Titan #69: Arthur Barrow

Arthur Barrow is a musician, composer, producer, and arranger. In 1978 he began playing bass in Frank Zappa's band.

Arthur Barrow at your service.
Photo by Angilee Wilkerson

Titan #70: Oneida James

Oneida holding down the groove. Photo by Rego Meijer

Oneida is best known for performing as bassist and background vocalist with the late, great Mr. Joe Cocker. https://www.oneidajames.com/bio

Titan #71: Daniel Miranda

Bassist for Queen + Paul Rodgers, Meat Loaf, and others, Daniel currently performs with Blue Öyster Cult and Bad Penny. https://www.facebook.com/Dannymiranda3; https://www.instagram.com/dbasmn/

Daniel Miranda played bass on Blue Öyster Cult's 1995 album *Curse of the Hidden Mirror* among others.

Titan #72: Wyzard

Wyzard's innovative style of playing-thumping-slapping the bass and his songwriting was greatly influential in what was to become funk rock. He wrote Mother's Finest's biggest hit, "Baby Love." https://wyzard.net/

When I started playing there was this band called Mother's Finest with this amazing bass player called Wyzard.

—JD Pinkus

My first bass hero was Wyzard from Mother's Finest. I remember at one show I was close to the front row. I was blown away by his playing and solos. Because of him I began to research other bass players like him.

—Kai Eckhardt

Wyzard grooves with purple bass.
Photo by Biggi Toast

Wyzard was very influential for me. He had the chops that he showed on his thumping Alembic. He also had great stage presence. I mean, he looked like a bass player.

—SHORTY B

Titan #73: Tony Green

Tony "T. Money" Green is an American bass player, record producer, and award-winning songwriter well known for his work with Death Row Records, Dr. Dre, George Clinton, Snoop Dogg, and Tupac.

Tony Green and his laid-back groove.
Photo by Steve Galli

Titan #74: Jim Pons

Born March 14, 1943, in Santa Monica, California, Jim Pons is a bass guitarist and singer who played for several 1960s rock bands including the Leaves, the Turtles, Flo & Eddie, and Frank Zappa's The Mothers of Invention. In 1973 Pons left the music business to become the film director of the New York Jets Football Club, which position he retired from in 2000. He now lives in Jacksonville, Florida, where he plays bass in a bluegrass band called Lonesome Ride.

Jim Pons, veteran bassist.
Photo by Henry Diltz

Titan #75: Mark Bedford

Mark in Madness. Photo by Aron Klein

Mark "Bedders" Bedford is a bassist and songwriter for the band Madness.

Titan #76: Rudy Sarzo

Rudy was a member of Quiet Riot at their most popular point, playing on albums like 1983's *Metal Health*.

Sarzo remains best known for his work with Quiet Riot, Ozzy Osbourne, and Whitesnake, and is currently the bassist for The Guess Who.

Day 8: "Future Titan of Bass" Challenge Action Step

1. Visit http://www.bassguitarbeginner.com for Day 8 of the challenge.
2. Visit the "Titans of Bass" Facebook group (details in "How to Use This Book" section).
3. Visit the YouTube channel (details in "How to Use This Book" section).

Play F Note and G Note

Now that we tackled the C note, find the other two notes that we are going to use—the F note and the G note. Listen to the song another three times and try to listen to the chord changes in the song.

The pattern doesn't change. It goes from F to C, then from G to C. It then repeats throughout the whole song. Let's locate all three notes and play them. As you know the C note from yesterday, we are covered there. Look at your Connect-the-Dots Adventure map and find the other two notes.

Go up one string to the D string. As you can see, the F note is directly above the C note—third fret and second string. The G note is two frets down—third string, fifth fret.

Today we are going to play all three notes. Practice the same exercise as yesterday with the C note. Use the index finger of your left hand to press down on the fret until you get a clean noise and strum the string with your right hand. Practice playing that one note, playing it over and over in ten-note intervals. Practice this in five-minute intervals, playing that note every three seconds.

Play the same exercise with the F note. Use the index finger of your left hand to press down on the fret until you get a clean noise and strum the string with your right hand. Practice playing that one note, playing it over and over in ten-note intervals. Practice this in five-minute intervals, playing that note every three seconds.

Play the same exercise with the G note. Use the index finger of your left hand to press down on the fret until you get a clean noise and strum the string with your right hand. Practice playing that one note, playing it over and over in ten-note intervals. Practice this in five-minute intervals, playing that note every three seconds. Keep at it—you are doing fine!

Tip: Listen to the downloaded "1: The Midnight Special—Bass Track" from https://www.bassguitarbeginner.com/ and the YouTube channel. Today, listen to the song with bass track three times all the way through. This will help you get used to the bass notes and melody.

ᗪ*ay* 9
Less Is More
Practice Chord Changes

Less is more. I'm sure you have heard that before. Is this a cliché, or does it mean something when it comes to bass and bass players?

Let's Ask the Titans: Is "Less Really More" When It Comes to Bass Playing?

If you can make something happen with less, it becomes much more interesting to the listener. It becomes something that they take more possession of. I greatly admired Andy Fraser of the band Free. He was great at leaving behind less in the song. Sometimes he didn't play through verses at all! The difference is like looking at a color photograph compared to a black-and-white one. A color photograph has everything shaded in, all the colors. It leaves nothing to the imagination. But with black and white, people will linger and look at it more intently. All the information has not been given to them. They have to fill in the colors for themselves.

It's the same idea with your playing. If you fill in most of the colors, you possess that unique view of the image, not the listener. If you leave things out, the listener is required to fill in the gaps. They will be more connected to it. It's easy to play fast and throw in a lot of notes.

You want to say things in the most effective and meaningful way possible, yet still allow some space for the listener to inject their own imagination into the song. You can imply things rather than play them.

—Phil Soussan

It's the notes that you don't play that matter more than the notes you do play.

—Billy Gould

Put the notes in the right place. Stop trying to fit twenty pounds of trash in a ten-pound bag.

—HARLEY FLANAGAN

There is no "bumper sticker" answer to the "less is more" question. It depends on the music, the moment, the sound, and the audience. The bass isn't a melodic instrument, yet if you hear a Beatles song, Paul McCartney is all over the fretboard. James Jamerson was a similar example in Motown. The bass was the most active instrument in the mix. So, we see the two most popular and loved bass players of all time and their playing wasn't "less is more."

—BILLY SHEEHAN

In most situations it is great to be told, "Can you play busier?" or "Can you turn up?" Those are both good signs regarding your playing. When you play certain types of music, it pays to be a good listener. I've recently played some pop country gigs. From a technical perspective, it wasn't that challenging from a technical aspect. It's not really about me or my bass part. You can change one little thing that makes the song either better or worse. For example, if you play a long note rather than a shorter note in certain areas. The nature of the bass instrument is that when you change something small, it can make a big difference in the song. It helps to think about the responsibility and power of the bass in the total effect of the song. It's good to practice a little less in the melodic fills that are needed. This is important in terms of being hired and being busy playing gigs and sessions. You can play tasteful yet simple techniques in 90 percent of all situations.

—JOSH COHEN

In rock music, bass players were busy and nobody complained. As a professional musician in the eighties, people were telling me to play less. This attitude never really got better. If you have a bass player that fills out the sound, you don't need a keyboard player or even a rhythm guitar player in the band. These days most bands just play what the guitar player is playing. But the bassline can really change the song.

—BJORN ENGLEN

I have been in sessions where I had to come and fix the bassline because the other bass player played too much. I came in and laid it down with the "less is more" idea and was successful.

—RUSSELL JACKSON

Less is always more. Usually, the less notes you play means the more you are really listening. If you play a lot of notes, you might be fighting against the singer and the guitar player. It's like trying to get out of the flow of traffic. Where are you going to go? You should stay with the traffic. If you play too much in the beginning, you have nowhere to go. When I play with Paul Simon on tour, I play very simply. Then if he wants more, I can always add more notes and try new things.

—Bakithi Kumalo

Less is more. There is a tendency to overplay and to show off. More often than not, it hasn't been welcome or sounded good in my experience. Less is more in everything, including life.

—Eva Gardner

The older I get, the less I tend to play. Also, the less I am thinking when I'm playing, the better.

—Julie Slick

Many times younger players try to focus on playing quickly. This can cause them to show off. As I get older, I appreciate when a bass player uses just one note in the right place. That note is just awesome right there. Look at a simple bass walk from one chord to another with the right notes and it feels great. There is something to be said about laying back when you need to.

—Michael Lepond

From a practical standpoint, it seems like that most times "less is more" in mainstream music. When people hire me to play on records, I start with less. They have the option to ask for more. It is safer to come to from a place where the bass is a foundational instrument. This leaves room for all the musicians to think and feel in the creative process.

—Adam Nitti

I treat the melody portion of the song more like it's singing. There are so many basslines out there that you probably won't remember them as chops. If you can remember the melody, then you are doing your job. Most of the time a bass player isn't a solo player.

—Wayne Jones

Less can be more, but sometimes you want more to be more. As with anything that you learn, you have to know when to use it, not just what to use.

—Victor Wooten

Less is more only if you have something to say that's worthwhile. You can play a lot of notes and licks, but it will have no meaning without feeling behind it. I'm with Luke Bryan's band in the country genre, so it's important not to be noticed that much. It has kept me employed. The song is the key so you don't want to be a distraction.

—James Cook

What makes a good bassline? It's true for any instrument, especially for the bass. The rests are important because they make the notes really count. Good basslines don't require gymnastics.

—Stu Cook

Less is always more, but less is less if you are boring. Like any Black musician that comes from the urban part of the country, you lay a groove down until everyone is hypnotized. Every now and then, you throw something in there that says "Wake up!" Then you quickly go back to playing the groove.

—dUg Pinnick

You have to play for the tune. You can't override or be really busy to drown out the vocals. You have to share holding down the bottom end and the groove.

—Jean Millington

Listen to your favorite hit pop song. The bass is never in the way of the other instruments. You have to listen to other parts before you jump in and plow through them. You are driving the car as the designated driver. You have to deal with the singer, egomaniac guitarist, crazy drummer, and the kooky horn section. You have to know who's in your car and get everyone to the end of the song safely. You are the one steering the car at all times. Yet, it's sort of in the background. In terms of physics, the bass sound takes up a lot of space. It has a large register. The smallest note can be huge on the bass. When a bass note comes in, it takes all the space, even if it's played softly.

—Gail Ann Dorsey

This also depends on the context of your playing. There is a subtle power to the bass—you can be more effective in playing very little. A classic example is when the bass plays the same riff, note for note. A famous session musician's advice was "think of something to play and play half what you first thought of." That was often the way things worked out for me when I was recording.

—COLIN EDWIN

Less is better sometimes. Generally speaking, people don't want to hear a super busy bassline. The bass needs to play its proper role. You shouldn't be playing a bunch of fancy stuff just to say, "Hey look at me! look at me!" It should be like a good film score. If it's there and you don't notice it, it's doing its job. I'm not a big fan of bass solos. I remember Frank talking about Patrick O'Hearn, who loved to take bass solos. Frank said he liked to "espresso" himself. Frank warned me about playing too busy. He said, "We are going to be playing in places like hockey rinks that are big and echoey. If you play a bunch of fast notes, they are going to be lost in the mush. Give some good solid bass notes, play a note that's long enough, that has time to fill the room. The lower the note is, the longer it takes to resonate.

—ARTHUR BARROW

It's not what you play—it's what you don't play.

—MARK BEDFORD

Learn the role of space, that less can be more.

—GEORGE PORTER JR.

It depends on the moment, not the song. When you listen to a recording, it's when people put down what the song actually needs. When you listen to a live recording, it's like hearing what people actually want to play. They are more spontaneous, they are in the moment, so they might play a really mad lick. It works in that moment, but if it was on the actual recording, it would get boring. A live recording band is the best of both worlds.

—GUY PRATT

Less is more is easily prescribed, but it's not always the right prescription. Oftentimes people are accused of playing too much when, really, they are not playing in time. Less is more helps if you are playing out of time. Simplicity can be amazing. But sometimes you want to contrast that with complexity and multilayered playing.

—ARIANE CAP

You don't need to say too much. It's low in the frequency spectrum, you hear it, and also you feel it too. When you make a noise, it carries a lot of weight sonically. The less you say, often the more people will listen to what you are saying. I remember people saying that I got more calls when I played less fancy. You need to leave space to let the other instruments sing and speak. It's like speaking—you don't talk all the time. But also when you are going to do a fill, say something good.

—BEN ELLIS

The art of spicing up things yet still leaving space is very hard to do. Pino Palladino does it beautifully. Anthony Jackson's playing wasn't always simple but he was always supported and served the music. Sometimes if you want to add a little more, you have to do it masterfully.

—HADRIEN FERAUD

A lot of young players tend to overplay a bit. It's not as cut and dried as "play simply and that's going to make you a better bass player." James Jamerson plays simply sometimes, but on many things he's moving quite a lot. Yet it's still grooving and functioning as a solid bassline. There's a time for all of it.

—DARRYL JONES

Before Devo, for a year and half I played bass with a band called 15-60-75 The Numbers Band. They were famous in Ohio, led by guitarist Bob Kidney. He was like Paul Butterfield but without being as famous as him. He was a real student of rural and urban blues. He would tell me to play less notes, just get rid of 25 percent of the notes I was playing. Just play on the beat. The bass has to be the driver. It's all about picking the right notes. The primal, hypnotic foundation has to be there. The drums and bass need to be locked. In Devo I loved playing with Alan Myers, a human metronome.

—GERALD CASALE

One of my teachers, Steve Swallow, told me that less is more because a bass solo is like a bear dancing. This can get very awkward. When a bear starts to dance, it has to be very careful with its movements. This is so people can discern and enjoy what you are doing.

—ABRAHAM LABORIEL

Herbie Flowers said, "Don't play too many notes." The more notes you play, the sound gets smaller, because our frequency is so big. Our search is always for the right notes, not the most notes. It's like a built-in "humble-izer." According to physics, you will end up being so small, you'll end up being a tiny little nothing that nobody can feel. A lot of bass is felt more than heard.

—Mike Watt

Space is really important. You need to develop a sense of where to play and where not to play. Some players use every opportunity to cram in a ton of notes. They try to impress with speed alone. This can be really unmusical and not always called for. Sometimes you need discipline as it's better to play nothing and leave behind complete space. It all comes down to taste and the music.

—Percy Jones

I wish I had paid even more attention to this adage when I was younger. Luckily, I was directed by Tommy LiPuma and Phil Ramone, guys who were both big producers in the charts, tell me parts in the song where "you can be a little free here with the bass." I would learn by finding out what they thought was correct in the song. It's an interesting style of music when you know the value of playing a whole note and leaving enough room for the vocals. I think I stuck to "less is more" about 80 percent of the time.

—Neil Jason

In pop music, many times we had to be super creative with as little notes as possible. We had to stay out of the way of the melody. We had to lock in the drums, stay away from the solos and the guitar parts. However, when it comes to improvised music, sometimes less is just less. With fewer players, sometimes you have to suggest something more. You need to give enough information or people won't know the tune. The problem with bass players is they play too much in the wrong situations. This can get you fired. I don't overplay because I'm trying to make room for other guys to shine. I like to think about what Ron Carter calls the "Big M" in music. This is the whole music, not just the individual bass parts. You have to think like a composer, not just on your part what you are doing.

—John Patitucci

It's not what you put in, it's what you leave out. As you mature you start to appreciate the stuff that Jerry Jermott and Carol Kaye did on records. Their bass parts are deceptively simple, but when you listen and try to play it, you see that they are doing a lot of stuff that's different. It sounds so simple that when you get used to it, that becomes the new normal.

—Klaus Flouride

It totally depends on the song. Look at James Jamerson on the song "(Your Love Keeps Lifting Me) Higher and Higher." He does something that most bass players wouldn't do. The song has those typical chord changes, but instead of following the chords with his bass pattern, he stays on the C chord throughout the whole song. In this way the chord changes have a lifting feel, which is perfect for the lyrics of the song. Only a bass player would notice this about the song.

On "Papa's Got A Brand New Bag," the bass sticks to the same riff throughout the song. The lack of any variation is hypnotic. The fact that he doesn't do any changes is what makes the song great. I also like stuff when the band lands on the chords and the bass might go right through the chord. On "No More Mr. Nice Guy" by Alice Cooper, during the verses, the guitar plays the same chord pattern. But on the second time around, the bass drops down a fifth, a step below the chords. It was a bold decision. I was always crusading for doing something different. We tried to make the song as exciting as it could be. We would always go a step beyond, take it to the limit, and then pull the reins in until we were doing our job supporting the song.

—Dennis Dunaway

I see myself as an economic player and the feel and groove aspect has always been more important to me than playing lots of notes or showing off. I hope to come up with melodic parts that benefit the song or tune. I have so many great memories playing with Jethro Tull—a great band that I was lucky enough to play with for many years.

—Dave Pegg

One of the most fun parts for me is to try and come up with appropriate basslines on simple tunes. When you are playing any instrument, you need to do what the music requires or what the competition is asking for. What does this song need? How can I make it better without showing off? If it doesn't need a really cool bassline line, then I don't do it.

—Dave Larue

My instrument has so much low end. If I'm not careful, I can overdo it. It's not just the notes, it's how to manage the frequency spectrum. Sometimes you can fill a space up with one fat note. I think it's better to err on less notes. Tony Levin does a great job of less is more. He plays an unusual less.

—TREY GUNN

Everything I've ever done is in the service of the song. Bass is like the complete skeleton, the chassis of the car. The lead guitarist is the flash body work, the drummer is the engine. The one thing that holds it all together is the bass—it ties the drums to the vocals. It's very top to bottom. The bass is in with drums and the vocal melodies. It also shouldn't get in the way by playing complementary countermelodies. You acknowledge what the voice is doing with phrasing and the correct choice of notes. When I did sessions, I tried to record the bass masters at the end, when the entire record was done.

—BRUCE THOMAS

It's a good thing to err towards. So often, especially when playing chords, so many bass players work out a way to play with the chords. Good bass players aren't afraid to make an interesting rhythmic fill with the root note and the fifth. You are still playing the chord, but when you do make an embellishment, it really makes the difference tonally. It's like what the great actor Michael Caine once said, "Your face is a huge thing on the big screen, so small movements make big results." The bass is such a seismic thing. Small movements make big differences. Bootsy Collins said, "Always hit the one." Funnily enough, my style often involves leaving out the one. The bass drum is like the skeleton and the bass is the elastic sinews that make the bones move of the body. I like to play a pickup note off the one as my first note. It's kind of like an elastic rhythm that you achieve by leaving the notes and the beat out of. You can make something hypnotic with half time aspects. In music you are always dealing with two things—sound and silence. Both have to be equally important and balanced. Silence turns into space. When you look at dub lines, they create a spacy world. This comes from silence and leaving space. The greatest bass players always have fantastic phrasing, like Aston "Family Man" Barrett. Phrasing is like when you give an actor three lines of script to see what he does with it. They can change it dramatically just by how they pause. It's the same with how dramatic you can be with phrasing. When you start a song and the bass comes in slightly lazy, almost too late, it can really leave you hanging. Even if it's only half a beat late. Miles Davis did this as a trumpet player. It makes the listener anticipate what's going on. It's like watching the Russian state circus with the trapeze artists. They push their act to the limits—it's always like someone is really going to fall down. It's very brave. It's like the phrasing of great actors. They know how to make a small change with things. Bass players have so much leeway that they might not realize, a lot of it just in the phrasing. By just using space, you can craft all kinds of phrasing combinations.

—JAH WOBBLE

Less is usually more. It reminds me of when I went to school for woodworking. They have the statement, "Measure twice, cut once." Less is more can be a humbling of oneself to what the song really needs. Sometimes in the arch of the song you might need to grab some attention—then you should play more. Most times I default to see what is the least that I can get away with. I play a lot of sixteenth notes.

—LIAM WILSON

Wow, that's certainly a lot of great information to ponder. Although we saw a lot of great and different ideas in there, what can we glean from it all?

In general, most of the Titans agree that "less is more." This means that you should be careful and be thoughtful of the notes that you play as well as the notes you don't play. You should always remember to serve the song with the drummers as the foundation of the rhythm section. Showing off or playing too many notes will usually not be appreciated by the rest of the band. It's important to really learn to listen so you play the bass in the way that you think the song needs.

This comes with practice and experience and listening to many different kinds of music. The subtle role of the bass player is to make the notes you don't play as important as the note you choose to play. Along with this, letting a whole note resonate on your bass can create a stronger statement than playing many notes.

Introducing the Titans: #77–84

Titan #77: Michael Lepond

Michael Lepond—heavy metal master.
Photo by Jatzi Nieto Photography

Michael Lepond—heavy metal bass player for Symphony X, Ross the Boss, and Mike LePond's Silent Assassins.

Titan #78: Basil Fearrington

Basil and his bass.
Photo by Bail Fearrington

Basil Fearrington—bass producer-composer-arranger. https://www.youtube .com/channel/UCNZ6HkoXMXg7K7sLPIP-RRg/featured

Titan #79: Bryan Beller

Bryan brings it. Photo by Drew Stawin

I try and play challenging material tastefully, with appropriate tone, for fancy guitarists and my own solo compositions alike.

—Byran Beller

Titan #80: Damian Erskine

Damian, the bass master. Photo by Cortney Erskine

Damian is primarily a touring bassist, and educator, author, and columnist. https://damianerskine.com; https://www.basseducation.com

Titan #81: Phil Soussan

Multifaceted Phil. Photo by Jim Wright

World-renown bassist Phil Soussan has been laying down the foundation upon which some of the greatest rock and roll has been built. Working with some of the biggest names in music, he has played with a who's who of artists, including Ozzy Osbourne, Jimmy Page, Billy Idol, Vince Neil, Johnny Hallyday, Steve Lukather, Edgar Winter, Richie Kotzen, and John Waite. As a songwriter, he has written for many of these artists, notably the megahit "Shot in the Dark" for Ozzy Osbourne. He is currently enjoying successes with the sensational rock band Last in Line.

Titan #82: Stephen Jay

Stephen Jay, bassist/composer. Photo by Ian Jay

Stephen Jay is best known for working with "Weird Al" Yankovic.

Titan #83: Steve Fossen

Steve Rocks out. Photo by Todd Hobert

Steve Fossen is co-founder/original bassist and 2013 Rock & Roll Hall of Fame member of Heart.

Titan #84: James LoMenzo

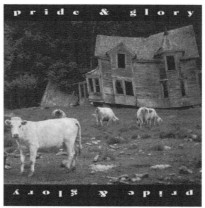

James played bass on the 1994 *Pride & Glory* debut album.

James LoMenzo was a member of Black Label Society, Megadeth, and Slash's Snakepit. http://www.jameslomenzo.com/

Day 9: "Future Titan of Bass" Challenge Action Step

1. Visit http://www.bassguitarbeginner.com for Day 9 of the challenge.
2. Visit the "Titans of Bass" Facebook group (details in "How to Use This Book" section).
3. Visit the YouTube channel (details in "How to Use This Book" section).

Practice Chord Changes (1) F to C and (2) G to C

Listen to the song with the bass notes. Listen to the song with the bass once. So now we are going to try to perform the chord changes needed for the song. This is F to C and then G to C.

Let's tackle the F to C change. The mechanics of this song is that we need to switch from playing the F note to the C in a short time. So let's practice playing the F note ten times, then a pause, and then we are going a string down to the C note—second string and third fret.

Play that note ten times and go back to the F note. Play ten times and go to C. Repeat ten times.

Now let's do the G to C change. We need to switch from playing the G note to the C note in a short time. Practice playing the G note ten times, then a pause, and then we are going down a string to the C note—second A string and third fret. Play that note ten times and go back to the G note. Play ten times and go to C. Repeat ten times.

That's the basic mechanics of the song. Practice the two main changes and we are more than halfway there. Awesome, keep it up!

Tip: Continue to listen to "1: The Midnight Special—Bass Track" that you downloaded. Today, listen to the track five times in its entirety. This will give your brain a chance to place the song in your "memory bank."

Day 10
Practice and Style

As you might remember, it's all about practice, practice, practice—the three Ps. How is your journey going? Do you think the bass is growing on you?

As we are well underway with learning "The Midnight Special" song, it's a good idea to get a little motivation on why there is no substitute for practice. If you have made it this far and have followed along, you now have had a little practice on the bass. Keep it up, you are doing awesome! It's not easy to pick up an instrument and play it, so I commend you.

As for practice, does this matter when we are learning the bass right now? Can you get away with not practicing, now or in the future? Let's see how practice and good habits can help with your playing.

The Titans Talk about Practice

Practice shows up in your playing immediately. When you practice, we can hear it—and when you don't, we can hear it.

—Stu Hamm

Every time you play, you are investing in the next time you play. It is never wasted. I have yet to hear a basketball player say he is going to "rehearse" shooting hoops. There is nothing wrong with practice. The real practice is playing in front of people, because it's the most real and scary.

—Mike Watt

Practice is what it boils down to. Learning scales isn't as important as doing what you like. Don't worry about what everyone else is doing—do what you like. If you are trying to copy someone else or imitate them, it's not as much fun as exploring different notes and patterns. I would rather sit down and invent a new riff instead of playing scales. If I was a studio musician, I would focus more on the scales and being as schooled as possible.

—Dennis Dunaway

Vince Lombardi said, "Practice doesn't make perfect. Perfect practice makes perfect."

—Shaun Munday

It's good for beginning bass players to keep your hand loose. You have to be strong and loose and relaxed all at the same time. Your hand has to be a certain shape. Most people have a longer middle finger than their index finger. When you pluck the strings, turn your index finger away from the body but your middle finger against the string so your fingers are the same length. Then you won't have to curve your hands with your picking finger. Tip your hand in and all of your fingers are available to every string. You need to master these things before you plug into the amp to get your own sound. Finding out how you can talk to the instrument and have the instrument talk to the world is the goal. For kids to know how to play bass and get better, 99 percent of them have to love the bass.

—Scott Thunes

A person only listens at the level of their maturity. It's like the icing on a cake. If you make a cake look beautiful, it's the icing that grabs your attention. It's easy to forget that that icing is really a razor-thin layer. But the most important part of the cake is the actual cake. I don't know of any chef that only makes icing. Your gift might be cake decorating, but you have to learn the boring part of how to bake a cake in order to learn the exciting part of how to ice it. Bass playing is definitely like that. We are 99 percent cake. We let the other instruments become the icing. When the music calls for us to step out, we want to be able to do that too. Our job might be considered boring to a lot of people. It's a lot of support; it's one note at a time with lots of whole notes.

My whole thing is to stand in the back and make you look better than you are. Even if you are great, if I'm behind you, you are going to be greater. That's an honorable role. I love it.

Just about all little boys when they get into music want to play drums and beat on something. I already was living with one of the greatest drummers in the world (my brother), so my family didn't need another drummer. I learned the drum solos on the bass as a kid. Back in the day, James Brown used to ask his band: "What instruments are you playing?" They would answer: "I'm playing a trombone, Mr. Brown." He would say "No, you are not." He then told them: "You are all playing the drums." This was because he wanted all the instruments in his band to have good rhythm. Even if you are playing a solo, you should be able to make people dance.

—Victor Wooten

Just for Fun! Don't Try This at Home!

I was with this musical project called the Wild Rats. It was with Mike Watt and Thurston Moore. When Mike Watt was in the studio, a tech just assumed that he should change all his bass strings, which he did. When Mike found out he was mad. He yelled, "Who changed my bass strings? I hate new bass strings!" He then ran up to this New York bagel spread that had lox in it. He grabbed a piece of smoked salmon and rubbed it vigorously all up and down the new bass strings. He then ate the salmon! I think it might be a secret technique. The salmon is the key. I never dared to try the technique but it's probably good for the wood—all those omega-3s. (laughs)

—SEAN LENNON

Let's Ask the Titans: What Does Style Have to Do with Your Playing?

As a former rhythm guitarist, I like to fill in the parts around a single guitar part, or play with the guitar to give a riff a heavier feel.

—GEEZER BUTLER

It just happens. I've never worked on style or tone.

—BILLY SHEEHAN

I know I have a style in the same way that I have a speaking voice. We never practice or work on our speaking voices, we just use it a lot. You are born with your style; you are already unique. As I've gotten older, I realize that my job is to make that voice better. I quit focusing on "being different" right away, but I did recognize what made me different. If you look for your "voice," you are looking for something you already have. When you can identify that, you can enhance it.

—VICTOR WOOTEN

I have more of a background style than say, Dennis Dunaway of the Alice Cooper band. He is often in front with his parts. The development of your style can depend on the people you play with and what your band is like. You really have to figure out what the band is about. It's the goal to try to get everyone on the same page. Make sure you know the people you play with and where you want to take music.

—JOE BOUCHARD

I think we're influenced by the music we listen to, too. I'd say I'm a rock/blues player with a love for country music. With time, we develop our own interpretation and style of playing. It's an ongoing process and often subliminal.

—LEO LYONS

What has kept me employed as a bass player is just playing the bass. The job of bass is to hold down the foundation with the drums. Any embellishments should add color and never get in the way of the rhythm. It can also be quite melodic as well. There is such range on the bass—the low and higher melodic ranges are pleasant to hear. Make sure you are playing the bass. Hold down foundation and don't get in the way of the song. Serving the song is the most important part.

—JAMES COOK

I loved an interview I read with Anthony Jackson and the way that he looks at the bass: "The electric bass is less related to the upright bass and more related to guitar. It's part of the guitar family." I completely agree with him. To clarify, it's part of the guitar family, just like rhythm guitar is part of the rhythm section also. It's multifunctional.

—RUDY SARZO

Maybe you can control your style. It's best not to worry about it too much. If you listen and are honest with yourself and if there's something you are doing you don't like, then ask "Why don't I like it" and try to understand. It takes place organically. When I was young, I just wanted to be Jaco. For a while, I didn't want to have my own style. I wanted to play like him. His style was all-encompassing and deep. There was so much to it. It seemed silly to develop another style for myself. I worked hard at playing his style. But I was nothing like him at all. I was a radically different person. I heard these things in my playing without trying or wanting to. I could usually play something like him. It was close but not perfect. That was me, not him. I turned the process around and worked on those things to see where they could go. It was a slow process and I made a lot of mistakes. When you develop musical things and they are not working out, you can work at it another way. It opens another door and so many interesting places to go.

—MICHAEL MANRING

When you really hear the music, you can see shapes and images. You can see every chord and textures. In some cultures, it's taught by following traditions. Some Romani musicians know scales upside down in every key, which means they usually worked on it upside down. They don't rely on licks at all. Licks are like a prison. Learn the chords, scales, and all the available tools. This is how you play the scales and show you how to create musical phrases.

—HADRIEN FERAUD

You have to play and copy other people's bass lines when you start. That itself is how you learn to play. You didn't make up the parts. You then play in an area of people who have done it before so you can develop chops. And even when you copy others' basslines, you won't play or remember it the same way as it was on the original. That's how you develop your style. Your way is different and just as viable. I still hear songs that I don't know who's playing on it. When I hear something new, I pick up my bass and then try to incorporate it in my playing. Style becomes part of your playing after many years. There are guys who just play jazz so they develop that style. There are famous rock players who might not have chops, but they influence millions of bass players. But to have that point of view is the most important part. I was lucky enough to be the bass player on Gene Simmons' (from Kiss) solo record. I was also lucky enough to be the bass player on Paul McCartney's Press to Play *album. We are talking about two vastly different bass players. You can't say that one is a better bass player than the other. They are both accomplished players for their specific mission and style. They are both really good at what they do. I didn't want to imitate Gene and Paul; they didn't hire me to imitate them. Gene Simmons said it "was too easy to play bass on his own record." You can't plan it. You can only hope it happens. You can try to develop your style with your interests. See where your personality leads you to. The more stuff you play, the more it helps develop your style.*

—NEIL JASON

It is important to first learn the structure and the importance of how a bass sits in a song. This is number one. Then as you go along, you can learn different styles. You will eventually find your own. This is what happened to me. I am a true rock player with a little jazz and a little boogie. It's more important to play correctly and to understand what bass is. The lucky ones do develop a style. Like Flea, Larry Taylor from Canned Heat, and

Jamerson, and, I dare say, me. Years ago I was featured in a Big *magazine poll that voted me second best in the world after Paul McCartney. That's pretty damn good. I do a bass and drum solo at my shows—it takes about fifteen minutes.*

—Suzi Quatro

You need to take liberties. You can be a little adventurous in your approach and the way you play the song. I have a recording studio in my house where people send me tracks that they want me to put the bass on. It's the feel and the feeling and where you place the accent in the track. It's your personality that develops over time where you can put your footprint on song.

—Kasim Sulton

You should focus on learning your instrument. This means learning all the notes everywhere on the fingerboard, playing in time, and being musically literate. I read music when I studied trumpet and piano—I was a sight-reader—but when I started playing bass, my ear did most of the work. Personal style comes after you've studied the styles of other great players. Then you develop your own.

—Stu Cook

You can't fall into it. It's like falling in love. You don't know you are in love until you are in love. Follow your heart and find stuff that you like to keep going. I don't know if it's that important. It depends on how far you want to take it. It can define you and you can be the best at it. Your style finds you through practice and passion.

—Brad Smith

You can't consciously develop your style. My style is a hybrid of all my influences. Here are my goals when I'm playing. I'd like to:

1. *Be as tight as Duck Dunn and always land on the money.*
2. *Be as melodic and inventive as Paul McCartney.*
3. *Be an important part of the recording like Jamerson.*
4. *Be a featured instrument like Entwistle.*

I like melodies, and originality. The main thing to remember is that you have to be on the one, as it were. An effective bass part doesn't depend on complexity or business. When you listen to "What Is Hip" by Tower of Power, it's a one bass-note phrase played in 16th notes. It's a good exercise for any bass player to try and play that line. If you're playing 16th-note bars regularly, the discipline of that would teach about 90 percent of what bass playing is about.

—BRUCE THOMAS

Style is the most important. It can happen by your limitations and turn into something else. I was playing fretless bass before Jaco. He took it to another level. You develop your own style on what you need to do. When it works, then people will notice. It's a journey to find out if style is going to work or not going to work.

—KENNY PASSARELLI

Your style happens organically. It's the sum total of everybody that you listen to your whole life. Sometimes I'll listen to one of my old records and realize where I got inspired from some of my riffs from. But a lot of it is you as you develop organically as you study. This also means working within your limitations.

—ROY VOGT

It's important to be heard. As a bassist in the late seventies, you were supposed to sit in the back and not be noticed. I started to try to change that. I bought chorus pedals and played up the neck and on the root of the neck. That was my style. When you hear me, you can hear that's Barry Adamson style. Playing up the neck became my trademark.

—BARRY ADAMSON

I am almost entirely self-taught. My mom paid a guitarist friend of mine for a lesson when I was starting out. He showed me how to tune, hold the bass, do a fingering exercise, showed me a blues chord progression, wrote out a scale and a riff or two. The rest has been playing, watching, listening to other players, and playing some more. About ten years ago, Flea showed me how he does slap bass. I practiced it over the next few years and have gradually integrated some of it into my style. I audited a music theory class in college which opened a lot of doors for me.

—CHUCK DUKOWSKI

Introducing the Titans: #85–94

Titan #85: Ronnie Dawg Robson

Ronnie talks with his bass. Photo by Mirella Ricci

Ronnie Robson is a professional session and touring bassist who has recorded with many well-known musicians and bands from around the world. www .ronnierobson.com

Titan #86: Scott Brown

Scott from Trooper. Photo by Scott Brown

Scott Brown is best known for being the current bassist of the Canadian rock band Trooper.

Titan #87: Harley Flanagan

Harley tears it up. Photo by Laura Lee Flanagan

Harley Flanagan is the founder and singer/bass player of Cro-Mags. He began playing drums with legendary New York punk-crossover pioneers, the Stimulators, in 1979 at the age of twelve. As a bass player, he is known for his percussive style, often noting that he plays bass like a drummer. www.harleyflanagan.com

Titan #88: Bunny Brunel

Bunny and his brilliant signature. Photo by Ash Gupta

Bernard "Bunny" Brunel has played with Chick Corea, Herbie Hancock, and Wayne Shorter. www.bunnybrunel.com

Titan #89: Kyle Eastwood

Kyle is a double bassist, composer, and producer. While continuing to develop his parallel career as a composer and arranger on his legendary father Clint's Oscar-nominated films *Mystic River*, *Million Dollar Baby*, and *Letters from Iwo Jima*, Eastwood has reaffirmed traditions while creating truly contemporary, lyrical, and melodic jazz. www.kyleeastwood.com

Kyle and his double bass.
©Kyle Eastwood

Titan #90: Monique Ortiz

Monique getting ready to play. Photo by Monique Ortiz

Monique Ortiz—front woman of Alien Knife Fight, A.K.A.C.O.D., and Bourbon Princess.

Titan #91: Michael Dempsey

Michael Dempsey has logged over forty-five years of listening, playing, studying, traveling with touring bands—including The 5th Dimension, The Sail, Vince Gill, Dan Fogelberg, Maria Muldaur, Ronnie Milsap, and many more artists. http://michaeldempseybass.com

Michael and his bass.
Photo by Elizabeth Hammer

Titan #92: Miki Santamaria

Miki walking on air. Photo by Bernat Almirall

Miki Santamaria is a professional bassist, producer, and educator from Barcelona, Spain. He has worked with many top productions, like *Rock of Ages* in the USA and the Spanish *Dancing With The Stars*. He is a worldwide touring master with a YouTube channel with over 190K subscribers. www.youtube.com/mikisantamaria

Titan #93: Mark Burgess

Mark takes the stage. Photo by David Schindler

Mark Burgess is bassist, lead vocalist, and principal composer with The Chameleons (UK), currently touring worldwide with ChamelonsVox. Mark continues to perform with fellow founding member of Chameleons Reg Smithies around the world. https://www.chameleonsmark.com/

Titan #94: Clint Conley

Clint from Mission of Burma.
Photo by Clint Conley

Clinton J. Conley is best known as the bassist and vocalist of Mission of Burma.

Day 10: "Future Titan of Bass" Challenge Action Step

1. Visit http://www.bassguitarbeginner.com for Day 10 of the challenge.
2. Visit the "Titans of Bass" Facebook group (details in "How to Use This Book" section).
3. Visit the YouTube channel (details in "How to Use This Book" section).

Now we are going to go over playing the song with what we have learned. We know that we go from F/C to G/C. Play the song without the bass notes and play along.

- Start playing the F note on the "Yonder come-a Miss Rosie" lyric. Practice strumming along to the F chord in steady F notes counting 1-2-3-4, 1-2-3-4. Play steady F whole notes in time with the song.
- When the chord changes to C, follow along and play steady C whole notes in time with the song.
- When the chord changes to G at the start of "Well, I know her by the apron and the dress she wore," play steady G whole notes at the same tempo as the F notes.
- When the chord changes to C, follow along and play steady C whole notes in time with the song.

Practice this along to the song five times from start to finish. Don't worry if you mess up or make mistakes. Do your best to listen to the song and play along rather than not making mistakes. Practice makes perfect so try to play the bass!

Tip: Please continue to listen to "1: The Midnight Special—Bass Track" another five times today. The more you listen to the song regularly, the easier it will be to play it later!

$\mathcal{D}$AY 11

The Bass Heroes of the Titans

Who are the bass heroes for the Titans? Who inspired them when they started and who inspires them now? Have they changed? I have broken the most popular choices down to their own categories. The most popular bass heroes were:

Jaco Pastorius

James Jamerson

John Paul Jones

Jack Bruce

John Entwistle

Paul McCartney

Chris Squire

Because of our huge tribe of Titans, I had to be economical with the heroes and space. I have created a top seven list of the most influential. I have abbreviated much of the info, but it was super interesting to see that most Titans were influenced by about twenty others. I appreciated every Titan's perspective and wish I could include more stories—I could write a book on this alone!

First, let's go down the list and then we will look at all the other bass heroes of our Titans!

Hero 1: Jaco Pastorius

Jaco is arguably the most famous bassist ever, certainly one of the most influential, and by far the most popular hero that was named in almost every interview. It was very cool to hear about many of the interviewees who knew him personally.

Without Jaco, where would we be?

—BRYAN BELLER

Jaco Pastorius inspired all of us.

—Manou Gallo

Jaco came along and changed people's perceptions on what you could actually do on the bass.

—Stu Hamm

I was a huge fan of Jaco Pastorius when I was a young man. I was more of a maniac, a disciple. I studied with him in New York in the eighties. I used to follow him around. They say, "Never meet your heroes." I wouldn't say it was a bad experience by any means. It was fun studying with him and spending time with him. He was an incredibly complex person. Who he could be on any given day could swing unbelievably. But with me, he was unbelievably sweet and kind. He used to love to play together a lot. You had to prod him a little to get some instruction out of him—in spite of that, he really loved teaching. I would solo, and then he would solo. He honestly enjoyed spending time with people. I want to remember him that way. He had a really big heart.

—Michael Manring

When I heard Jaco for the first time, I had to stay up all night until I learned out where all the harmonics were on the bass. He was one of the busiest players that I have ever heard and he overplayed a lot, but nobody cared because it felt so good. His rhythm, note choices, and techniques were all so good.

—Victor Wooten

I grew up in Miami and Fort Lauderdale. I knew Jaco well; he was a year older than me. We used to go out to the 4 O'Clock Club in Fort Lauderdale. It was a great time growing up and watching players at that time. Jaco told me something about playing: "You just pound on the one." When I was playing the early Mother's Finest gigs, I got so much joy just pounding on the one! I could play melodic stuff but I love playing a hard groove!

—Wyzard

Jaco came to a gig I was playing at back in the day. I didn't really want to talk to him. I've heard so many stories about him. He was a hero of mine. I didn't want to get blown away by something weird. Then he came up to me after the show. He told me to come to the back room with him. I thought "Gosh"—I'm not sure what was going to happen. He pointed at me and said, "You play beautifully." That was a highlight of my career for me. Jaco was like my generation's god. He changed the whole bass world, putting it right on its head.

—Marc van Wageningen

Warning: "Naked with Jaco Story!"

My girlfriend Charlotte always makes fun of me. When I just got a fretless electric 4-string, I was trying to figure out the technique. It was summer so I had my shirt off and I was sweating. I was playing along to these Jaco videos. She walked in on me and said, "Oh my God! What are you doing?" I said, "Nothing, I'm just practicing." She's like, "That's just really weird"—because Jaco didn't have a shirt on and I didn't have a shirt on and I'm all sweating. She's like, "What are you doing here?" I was also in the park. I said, "Nothing! I'm just practicing." It was kind of a "Naked with Jaco" moment.

It's hard to shred and not show off, but Jaco was great at it. Look how he played on the Joni Mitchell records. He's shredding but somehow, with his master class level, he flies around with Joni Mitchell's voice like the most beautiful little bird. That sounds easy, but it's really hard to do.

—Sean Lennon

I knew Jaco. He was a pretty complicated guy. I played with him a couple times and it scared me to death. The way I learned to play like Jaco Pastorius was when I bought a ticket to see the Weather Report in 1977. They didn't have a whole lot of bouncers because it was a college gig. I sat ten feet in front of him on the floor and watched him and thought, "Oh, he's putting his hand like that. If I go home and put my hand on the jazz bass like him, it will give me his sound." I figured out some of his stuff already, but it showed me how his fingering worked. A friend of mine introduced me to him after the concert, and I told Jaco, "Thank you for the bass lesson, that was great." He said, "That was a lesson in being tired. I was really tired." Jaco was a really casual guy.

—Roy Vogt

Jaco Pastorius was unbelievable. After seeing Alphonso Johnson with Weather Report, I bought a fretless bass. This was before "Black Market" came out. When I heard it, I was blown away. I saw the Weather Report three times, including once in Sweden in 1977. The Swedish crowds were very polite and quiet. After a few songs, I was getting annoyed because I couldn't hear the bass. I waited til it got quiet after a tune and I yelled out, "Turn up the bass!" and Jaco heard me from the stage. When they started the next tune, Jaco walked out to the front of the stage and listened to the house PA. He motioned to the mixer to indeed turn up the bass. I hung around because I wanted to meet him. He was very nice. I told him I was the guy that yelled to turn up the bass and he smiled. I shook his hand. Now, I have pretty big hands but my hands were swallowed up by his—they were huge! He was friendly and outgoing and kind of crazy at the same time.

—Arthur Barrow

What did Jaco always say? "When the ship is sinking, women and rhythm section first?"

—Wayne Jones

As I got a little older, I became aware of Jaco. It helped shape me as a bass player as an adult rather than when I was a kid. He displayed the potential of what the bass really was, like a solo melodic, instrument, like a cello. A favorite memory of mine was playing Madison Square Garden with Joe Satriani years back. I had seen Jaco play there with the Weather Report a year earlier. So when I walked on that stage, it was a really cool vibe for me because Jaco was just there.

—Dave Larue

I was from a small town called Starkville, Mississippi. There was a backstage music store where I would go to get records. A guy who worked there called Bird was an accomplished bass player. He made me a cassette mix tape when I started playing bass. Most of it was Jaco; he told me that I had to listen to him because he was great. Jaco influenced me heavily. I heard "Portrait of Tracy" and was inspired. The song influenced me when creating the Blind Melon song called "Toes Across the Floor." Hearing Jaco gave me permission to do what I wanted and realize there were no rules.

—Brad Smith

My famous Jaco quote is when someone asked Jaco, "Where did you get your sound?" He just held up his two hands.

—Christian McBride

The defining moment in my bass journey was when I was twelve and I discovered Jaco.

—Hadrien Feraud

Jaco was always a big part of my family's musical life.

—Damian Erskine

Jaco created a new style when it was needed. He created beautiful sounds. He could sing with a bass, it was like a voice.

—Bakithi Kumalo

Hero 2: James Jamerson

A very close second to Jaco, Jamerson's playing style is arguably more influential to the average bass player than Jaco's complicated phrasing. Also mentioned in almost every interview, Jamerson's playing on so many timeless Motown hits will be influential for many generations.

James Jamerson Senior came into a club I was playing many years ago. James had grown up with my mother-in-law, Martha Jean "The Queen" Steinberg in Detroit, a very famous DJ who actually named The Funk Brothers. I met him on my own in the Chitlin' Circuit in Compton. He had sat in front at a couple of gigs and watched me after James moved to LA. I didn't know who he was, but I thought he might be a musician because of how he was watching me. I came off the stage on the third night and he said, "I just want to tell you, you are really doing it. You're cutting the gig. For a white boy, you are pretty good. But, you know what, don't go above the sixth fret. Stay below in the first and second positions and don't play all that slap and fill stuff. Stay down low and be the foundation. Other than that, you are doing a good job.

Eventually, he brought his son down, James Jamerson Jr. We ended up doing a bunch of sessions and hung out together. I used to hire him at the China Club in Hollywood, and we used to do Motown Tribute nights. It was really cool to meet him on my own. That was an incredible experience.

—Kenny Lee Lewis

Back in the day, I didn't know James Jamerson's name. Motown didn't put any credits on their records. I met Anthony Jackson in 1973 when he was playing in the Billy Paul band with my brother. Jackson and Jamerson became my first heroes, and still are to this day. The tones of Jackson and Jamerson are the foundation of what I like to think that I'm about.

—Basil Fearrington

I think there is value to simplicity. James Jamerson had really innovative basslines but it wasn't complicated and based on flash. There weren't dig-me lines. It was so right for the music.

—NATHAN EAST

Go on YouTube and look up songs that have James Jamerson in them. Let the YouTube algorithm bring you all his tunes. Start playing as many as you can. He played on over two hundred top ten songs! All of us bass players owe a lot to him.

—MIKE WATT

James Jamerson was my first bass hero.

—KERN BRANTLEY

James Jamerson changed the world with his playing, even influenced Paul McCartney. We were all in a tribute book to him called Standing in the Shadows of Motown, *predating the movie by decades. Ron Carter, one of my heroes and friends, talks about how if you change the bass notes, you shape the music; little variances affect the overall sound of the music. The rhythm in the music carries all the harmonies; there are no melodies or harmonies without rhythm—the bass and drums.*

—JOHN PATITUCCI

James Jamerson is a must!

—ONEIDA JAMES

Jamerson was my absolute hero—nobody does basslines like him. He was very inventive and very organic. I play a little like him. I have been told by musicians who I have worked with, "Whatever you play is always correct"—which to me is a huge compliment.

—SUZI QUATRO

Some people have these ideas on what they think the bass playing goal for me is. Fortunately, nobody tried to do that for James Jamerson. When I ended up recording with Wayne Kramer for an album, he would always give his bass players a Bible made of song transcriptions of the James Jamerson style. He was from Detroit so, even though he was a punker and rocker, that's what he envisioned the bass to be. I never got one because he had given them all away—I had to get one at the store.

—SCOTT THUNES

Hero 3: John Paul Jones (Led Zeppelin)

John Paul Jones—I got to work with him in the past and he was amazing. Forget just a good bass player, but an incredible musician. He was the secret sauce of Zeppelin, no doubt.

—TREY GUNN

JPJ was everything to me when I was in middle school and he still is.

—TONY SAPUTO

John Paul Jones makes me want to practice. How many times have you heard "Dazed and Confused" thinking you know how to play it, but then you hear it again and there is a different nuance, every time!

—MARY HUFF

I'm a huge Jamerson fan and it seems apparent that JPJ was too. He had a unique pocket, but with a melodic Motown sentiment.

—ANGELINE SARIS

He provided a warm blanket under the band but he's really doing whatever he wants to do. He took a lot of liberties but none of it was overplaying. It always fit into the song.

—DANIEL MIRANDA

[Led] Zeppelin II was a big influence to listen more to improvisations and instrumenta-tions. "The Lemon Song"? He is improvising it the whole way—it opened my eyes.

—DAVE LARUE

Every single piece of his music was melodic, groovy—he could also play tight and clean.

—SCOTT THUNES

The first time I tried to play like a bass player was because of John Paul Jones. I still play a Jazzmaster because I saw him playing one.

—SEAN LENNON

Hero 4: Jack Bruce

My main inspiration was Jack Bruce. He was the first bass player that I saw up close at a club in Birmingham. I had gone to see Cream, specifically for Eric Clapton. His playing on John Mayall's Bluesbreakers' album was groundbreaking. I was mesmerized with the stuff that Jack Bruce was doing on bass. He bended the strings and played totally avant-garde bass runs and riffs. He was almost playing lead guitar on bass.

—GEEZER BUTLER

Jack Bruce's role in the Cream power trio was like having all the freedom you want as long as you are doing the job of being a bass player, not the lead player or soloist. When he plays the least, it gets me off the same as when he plays the most.

—DANIEL MIRANDA

He was able to sing vocal melodies and play root notes creatively while still driving the song. In Cream, I thought he was more creative than Eric Clapton was.

—GERALD CASALE

He's a great musician and one of my biggest influences. Cream was the first rock group I got heavily interested in. I love their music to this day.

—CHUCK DUKOWSKI

His bass playing is just ungodly, amazing, constantly inventive.

—CLINT CONLEY

He came along and changed my whole musical life with his brilliant playing.

—JEFF BERLIN

Back in the day I got an 8-track tape of a Cream anthology. Jack Bruce was the first guy where I could tell and hear what the bass player was doing.

—MIKE WATT

Hero 5: John Entwistle (The Who)

I was staying at John Entwistle's house in England one time. We were there for a few days as my dad was the bassist in the band called The Creation. He let me borrow one of his basses for the time that I was there. He called me into his home studio—him and my dad were hanging out. I was only a teenager at the time; I was only fifteen. He called me into the studio, and said, "Hey, check out this Buzzard bass." He put it around my shoulders. It was way too big for me and hung way too low. Look, even the eyes lit up. It was a really, really cool moment where we were just hanging in the studio, and he made me feel included and encouraged. I look back now and realize how pivotal that was for me to feel supported and encouraged as a kid. I couldn't really appreciate who he was at the time. He was just one of my dad's lunatic friends. They were all just raving mad, all these incredible artists who were true innovators. I really didn't appreciate the gravity of that at the time until later. What I did realize was that he was totally instrumental and encouraging to me as a young person. That was huge. Just him saying, "Have a little play on the bass" in the studio. That was enough for me to feel like part of the gang.

—Eva Gardner

About ten years ago, I started playing with Roger Daltrey and The Who. I discovered Entwistle and got into his songs. I learned sixty to eighty of his songs and became a real fan. It's in my bones now. I'm really awed by his talent. It changed my attitude and my bass playing in a good way. I now have a much bigger palette to choose from.

—Jon Button

The bass gives the music its color, especially in a three-piece band. My yardstick for bass playing back when I was with the Sex Pistols was John Entwistle. We used to do a cover of "Substitute" in the Sex Pistols. That low bassline part was fantastic. Any bass player should check out what he does in the song "My Generation." The guitars are going one way and the bass counterpoints it and swings the melody.

—Glen Matlock

I saw John Entwistle use a pick, fingers, and slap all in the same tune!

—Mike Watt

John Entwistle had a very trebly bass tone that really cuts through. He said that he "was playing like a surf guitar player."

—Rob Stoner

When Entwistle came along, it was like "Wow, this is a whole new level, like bass on steroids."

—Gerald Casale

Hero 6: Paul McCartney (The Beatles)

When I was playing for Paul (on his solo 1986 record Press to Play*), there was a song we were playing, and we got to the bridge, and I just couldn't think of anything—I was thinking too hard. Like, what could I play that was interesting that would be like Paul, or make him look over and say, "Yeah, that's it" or "What would Paul McCartney do?" So I went and sat down next to him at the piano and said, "Y'know we get to this section . . ." We were all frustrated about a certain thing on that song. I said, "We get to the section and I'm not too sure what to play." He stopped. He was dealing with his own keyboard part at the time and he looked over at me and said, "Well, if I really knew what to do in that section, I would bloody well play it myself now, wouldn't I?" And for a second I went, "Oh shoot, of course!" and I thought, "What the heck did I just say?" And I slinked back into my little corner and I said, "Stop thinking and start playing the music that he's writing." I think we got in on the next take because I thought, "Yeah, that's right. This is a regular session." It was hard not to look over at Paul McCartney and go "holy crap!" But after a few days, you realize that "holy crap" isn't going to get the job done. You had better pay attention and play the basics, play the song and support the chords. He was a great father, husband, a very nice guy, a friend to everyone in the band.*

—Neil Jason

When I worked with Paul McCartney, he was the nicest man in the world. We were only in the studio for four or five hours. The fact that he recorded live with us was very impressive. I know so many megapop legends that are so accustomed to singing with tracks in the studio. Even if they do live vocals, they do scratch vocals and come back and put on real vocals later. Sir Paul came and recorded live with us. From what I remember of him singing, when I heard the recording, it was the same thing. Whatever his vocals were at the session, he used it on the record. He's a super nice man too.

—Christian McBride

Paul McCartney was such a prominent bass player. Paul played the bass and my dad didn't play the bass, so I always associated it with Paul. I find it amazing when I look at Paul playing a funky bass line while he is singing. Paul said this about the Beach Boys. "Listening to the Beach Boys made me realize that you don't always have to play the root note on the bass. If you don't do that, then you can find more interesting basslines."

—Sean Lennon

I read some articles and a lot of times Paul was able to do the bass tracks at the end of the recording process, which let him play what he wanted to. In a lot of the Beatles songs, the bass is really busy but it's amazing how good it feels. I know Paul was influenced by James Jamerson and all those Motown guys.

—WYZARD

The Beatles were the first band that got me into music, largely because of Paul's playing. It's ironic that the greatest band in rock and roll were also one of the first real bands— amazing how high the bar was set by the Beatles and their songwriting.

—DAVE LARUE

Paul McCartney was my first hero as I'm a massive Beatles fan.

—PETE TREVAWAS

Paul McCartney was the first as he was more inventive in an individual approach. How he played the countermelodies and sang was amazing.

—DENNIS DUNAWAY

Paul McCartney had to play bass when they started. He had no sense of the rules about being a bass player. He just picked it up and started playing it. I heard he wasn't that happy about it at first.

—MICHAEL MANRING

Hero 7: Chris Squire (YES)

This was in the nineties with Mother's Finest. We did a record called Black Radio Won't Play This Record. *We were doing a show at the Roxy in Hollywood. After the sound-check, I went to the Thai restaurant to order some food and sitting in the restaurant was Chris Squire, sitting by the window with this woman. I told Dion the drummer, "Hey man, that's Chris Squire, I'm going to talk to him." So I went over there without thinking about it and I just said, "Chris you are such a big hero. I'm playing in a band called Mother's Finest." And the women across from him said, "Mother's Finest—Chris, that's my favorite band!" I said, "We are playing tonight and you are welcome to come," and she said, "Chris, we gotta go." I put their names on the guest list. My guest list that night was Chris Squire plus one. As we were playing the show, I was hoping he would show up. It was a great show—Herbie Hancock and all kinds of cool people were there and the place was packed—the Roxy in Hollywood. I was doing a bass solo that was long and extended; I got to go crazy. I had my eyes closed. Then I opened my eyes and standing right in front of me was Chris Squire! He had made his way all the way to the front of the stage, and he was standing there watching me play with this smile on his face. I could have died right there because life was complete for me. He was such an innovator—the tone, the phrasing, the groove.*

—Wyzard

I became really good friends with Chris Squire many years after I started playing music. It took a while for me to really appreciate his sound and playing and his contributions. I never looked at his bass playing as an influence until many years later.

—Phil Soussan

Chris Squire was definitely the guy who got me wanting to be a bass player. I heard a "Roundabout" by YES on the FM radio. I got my first bass in 1973.

—Stu Hamm

When I heard his tone, it changed everything. It reminded me of a grand piano bass tone.

—dUg Pinnick

Chris had a brilliant sound, high pitched and thick bottom combination. I think it was the first time I heard anything like that.

—Jeff Berlin

Other Heroes

Other popular choices include Donald "Duck" Dunn, Stanley Clarke, Bootsy Collins, and Carol Kaye. For brevity, most of these mentioned here aren't mentioned below; here are some other interesting choices.

The four cornerstones of bass for me are—Duck Dunn for soul, Jamerson for funk, McCartney for pop, and Entwistle for rock.

—Bruce Thomas

Duck Dunn was a dear friend and the prime influencer of my style. Back in the sixties when CCR was playing at the Royal Albert Hall in London for the second time, Tony Joe White was our special guest, and Duck Dunn was the bass player in his quartet. Jim Marshall, a famous rock photographer, was with us to document the tour throughout Europe. He was an obnoxious guy, but you still wanted to have him around. He took it well when we busted his balls. We were winding each other up before the show, and Marshall bet me $100 that I couldn't get Duck Dunn to walk onstage at Royal Albert Hall and take his Duncan Yo-Yo and do an "around the world" trick during our set. We offered Dunn $50 of the $100 to do the trick. During our set, almost on cue, Dunn went onstage with his Yo-Yo, did the trick and exited stage left. Getting the $100 from Marshall was a real joy and a great memory.

—STU COOK

I met Stanley Clarke when I was nine. He became one of my first real bass heroes.

—VICTOR WOOTEN

Paul Chambers, Ron Carter, Dave Holland, Oscar Pettiford.

—KYLE EASTWOOD

Elvis Presley's bass player Bill Black. Ray Brown, Scott LaFaro for jazz.

—LEO LYONS

Willie Dixon. Bernard Odin (James Brown) played a lot of funky lines that were copied so much. A record featuring Eddie Gomez had an incredible solo that showed me it was possible.

—BUNNY BRUNEL

I was aware of Sting—the Police records had this upfront bass. Mark King brought the bass in the forefront. Pino Palladino.

—COLIN EDWIN

One electric bass player named Cliff Barton—he played with Georgie Fame and the Blue Flames. Charles Mingus was a huge influence.

—PERCY JONES

Charlie Mingus, Charlie Haden, Scott LaFaro, Ray Brown, and Stevie Wonder's left hand on that Moog organ.

—LIRAN DORI

Marcus Miller for his bass melody. Victor Wooten for the work he did rhythmically. Richard Bona or Daniel Romeo; Benoît [Vanderstraeten] for technique.

—MANOU GALLO

Anyone who plays acoustic bass who is determined to make it do something really personal.

—RON CARTER

Mike Kerr from Royal Blood has a very innovative and unique bass style.

—GEEZER BUTLER

Paul Samwell-Smith from the Yardbirds; Tim Bogert from Vanilla Fudge.

—BILLY SHEEHAN

Oteil Burbridge, Victor Wooten, Flea, Casandra Faulconer, Nick Daniels, Tony Hall, and Bobby Vega.

—GEORGE PORTER JR.

Bill Wyman, Ronnie Wood's playing on Jeff Beck's Beck-Ola.

—KASIM SULTON

Charles Mingus, Ray Brown.

—JACK CASADY

Les Claypool was one of my teachers when I was a kid. Charles Mingus' Black Saint and the Sinner Lady *is my favorite bass player's composed album. Tina Weymouth, Michael Henderson who played with Miles Davis.*

—SEAN LENNON

Steve Harris from Iron Maiden, Joey DeMaio from Manowar. Geddy Lee. I would listen to Ritchie Blackmore on guitar and try to transpose it to bass.

—MICHAEL LEPOND

As a teenager, it was Cliff Burton. I not only loved his playing, but also the way that he seemed to be totally consumed by the music in a totally sincere way.

—JUSTIN CHANCELLOR

One of the most underrated players was Dickie Peterson from Blue Cheer, in terms of songwriting, bass playing, and really how big they sounded. Mel Schacher from Grand Funk [Railroad]. Tony Maimone from Pere Ubu.

—JD PINKUS

Ray Brown, Eddie Gomez.

—BLAISE SISON

Holger Czukay (Can) taught me the value of octaves and when to switch. Klaus Voormann—a great bass album is the first Plastic Ono album—plays bass like somebody who's a graphic artist. Trevor Bolder from the Spiders from Mars.

—GLEN MATLOCK

Tom Kennedy helped me start. Anthony Jackson, Flea, Jimmy Johnson, Andrew Gouche, Joel Smith.

—BUBBY LEWIS

Other than my dad, James Jamerson, any James Brown bassists, Fred Thomas, Charles Sherrell, Paul Chambers, and Ray Brown.

—CHRISTIAN MCBRIDE

Oscar Pettiford, Wilbur Ray, Ray Brown Jr., Richard Davis.

—ABRAHAM LABORIEL

I love Gerald Veasley, Meshell Ndegeocello, Chuck Rainey, Zander Zon, Josh Cohen, Victor Wooten.

—ARIANE CAPE

Your heroes are always those playing popular music when you are trying to play popular music. For me it was Bill Wyman of the Rolling Stones.

—GERALD CASALE

Bill Wyman: The Stones' sound was more a big blend and the bass was a unifying sound. The Yardbirds—Paul Samwell-Smith was equally as innovative as Beck or Page. He taught me that I could do anything I wanted to with a blues pattern, which opened up my whole style.

—DENNIS DUNAWAY

Dennis Dunaway took me to see Stanley Clarke live. We went to Toad's Place in New Haven. The first thing in the show is he jumps off the stage and lands on the tables and starts playing the bass. He played for an hour, all bass solos, and it just seemed like ten minutes. He's one of my heroes. I ended up buying an Alembic bass because he played one. I played the solo on "Godzilla" with it.

—JOE BOUCHARD

Ray Brown, Charles Mingus, and then the Beatles came along. Carol Kaye and Joe Osborn were playing everybody's music. They were people I was looking for as examples of the kinds of parts that I'd like to be playing without originally knowing who they were.

—LELAND SKLAR

The memory of seeing Bootsy Collins at seventeen playing "Sex Machine" was really quite incredible, playing that one riff over and over. Despite everything he's done since, which is absolute pure brilliance. JJ Brunell from The Stranglers' Rickenbacker sound is unique. The way I played in Magazine—using the thumb, mute with the palm, and doing other tricks—was due to Larry Graham.

—BARRY ADAMSON

I would try to play some of the grunge stuff, like Krist Novoselic (Nirvana), Jimi Hendrix—Noel Redding. I love Jeff Ament in Pearl Jam, some of the fretless stuff, so I actually bought one.

—MARK STOERMER

Marcus Miller, Victor Wooten.

—SHAUN MUNDAY

My teachers were on records: Marcus Miller, Gary Willis.

—SHEM SCHROECK

Tony Levin inspired me to get into the Chapman Stick, which is really the instrument I'm best known for. Sting, Geddy Lee, Cliff Burton.

—Tom Griesgraber

I ended up in a new wave band called the Readymades in the seventies. They gave me a Joe Jackson record to check out the bass player, Graham Maby. He is still one of my favorite bass players but I didn't play like him. Nowadays I like JJ Brunell from the Stranglers; he's like the modern-day Chris Squire.

—Scott Thunes

Meshell Ndegeocello, Richard Bona, Tim Lefebvre, Anthony Jackson, Tony Scherr, Charlie Haden, Dave Holland, Scott LaFaro.

—Gina Schwarz

Larry Grenadier, Miroslav Vitous.

—Jasper Høiby

My first was Flea.

—Henrik Linder

Chuck Rainey. Pino Palladino is great on fretless bass. Wilbur Bascomb—from New York City—he played on the original film version of Hair *made in 1978. He's got an incredible style unlike anyone I've heard.*

—Gail Ann Dorsey

Early on I was a big fan of Stevie Ray Vaughan and Double Trouble. I love Tommy Shannon's playing.

—James Cook

Stanley Clarke, Chuck Rainey, George Benson, Steely Dan, Al Jarreau.

—Bakithi Kumalo

The ones that shaped my style of playing were Lemmy from Motörhead and Darryl Jenifer from Bad Brains, Felix Pappalardi from Mountain, Rainy [Roy Wainwright] from Discharge, Cronos [Conrad Lant] from Venom.

—Harley Flanagan

There are incredible players like Pino Palladino, Tony Levin, Tina Weymouth.

—JOAN ARMATRADING

Andy Fraser from Free: I'm still trying to figure out some of his lines. Then Willie Dixon, Tommy Shannon, and Keith Ferguson.

—HORACE PANTER

JJ Burnel from the Stranglers was one of the first that made a bass that sounds like a guitar. Kim Deal from the Pixies. Kim Gordon from Sonic Youth—she was doing stuff no one else was doing.

—BEN ELLIS

My favorite bass hero is Johann Sebastian Bach. I was a piano player and I took classical piano lessons as a kid. I noticed the left-hand parts on JS Bach recordings in transcriptions were very challenging. Some others have also noticed that these left-hand JS Bach compositions are the beginnings of modern bass playing. If you divide it up in an attractive way, use good chord substitutions, and have a counterpoint melody line on the left hand to what the right hand of the keyboard is doing, you essentially have the rules of bass playing as we know it today.

—ROB STONER

Flea, Marcus Miller, Pino Palladino, Victor Wooten, Nathan East, Gary Willis.

—MIKI SANTAMARIA

Anthony Jackson, Marcus Miller, Chuck Rainey, Willie Weeks, Ray Brown, Verdine White, Flea, Jimmy Haslip, Meshell Ndegeocello.

—ONEIDA JAMES

I heard Van Morrison's live album It's Too Late To Stop Now *with bass player David Hayes and learned every lick of it. Andy Fraser (Free), Bruce Thomas, Aston Barrett, Tina Weymouth, and Joe Dart (Vulfpeck).*

—MARK BEDFORD

Mark King (Level 42), Victor Wooten, Les Claypool, Marcus Miller, Stu Hamm.

—SCOTT BROWN

Early on Gene Simmons of Kiss, Ian Hill of Judas Priest, and Cliff Williams of AC/DC, Steve Harris (Iron Maiden), Neil Murray (Whitesnake).

—BJORN ENGLEN

George Porter Jr.

—BRAD SMITH

When I was learning, Stanley Clarke, Dee Murray (Elton John's band). These days Philip Bynoe, Victor Wooten.

—JAMES LOMENZO

The first guy I really noticed was Larry Graham, a huge hero of mine. I got a chance to meet him when he was on the bill with Spyro. He showed up for soundcheck in his full white suit, looking like he was in the show. I met him, and I told him, "If there were no you, there would be no me."

—SCOTT AMBUSH

John Deacon from Queen. Chuck Wright from Quiet Riot.

—DAVEY RIMMER

Ray Brown, Jerry Jermott, Geddy Lee, Phil Lesh, Jack Casady, Flea, Sting changed the whole way of thinking and feeling about the instrument. Stevie Wonder's synth bass playing.

—DANIEL MIRANDA

Larry Graham and Stanley Clarke (Return to Forever) and the solo were the first time I really listened to music and thought—this is my music; my dad was jazz and my mother was soul.

—DARRYL JONES

Duck Dunn. He was my first, so accessible; he played with a rudimentary element that was within my grasp at first. Chuck Rainey: I actually took lessons with him when I was seventeen for a little while.

—DAVEY FARAGHER

Aston "Family Man" Barrett. His lines were very musical because Bob Marley wrote proper songs. He had a relaxed, Jamaican phrasing style but also had to remain true to the chords of the tunes. I saw him play at the Lyceum with Bob Marley on July 18, 1975. That was the best gig I ever saw.

—Jah Wobble

Michael Anthony from Van Halen.

—Derek Frank

The bass player on Buddy Miles' live album in '71 or '72 (David Hull)—he was like James Jamerson and Willie Weeks all wrapped up in one, but could play faster, he had a scary pocket.

—dUg Pinnick

Introducing the Titans: #95–104

Titan #95: Marc van Wageningen

Marc and his bass. Photo: Tina Abbaszadeh

Marc "VW" van Wageningen, bass player with the Tower of Power, is also a composer and solo artist. https://towerofpower.com/marc-van-wageningen

Titan #96: Joshua Cohen

Josh Cohen is a multi-award-winning bass-ist who is best known for his use of extended techniques—namely two-hand tapping—to create the sound of an entire band with only one instrument in real time. www.themusic ofjoshcohen.com

Joshua Cohen, bass titan.
Photo by Alice Xue

Titan #97: Davey Faragher

Davey played bass with Cracker from 1990–1993, like on their 1992 self-titled debut album.

Davey Faragher was a member of Cracker, and worked with John Hiatt's band. He has also worked with the Imposters, the backing band for Elvis Costello since 2001.

Titan #98: Jasper Høiby

Jasper and his double bass. Photo by Dave Stapleton

Copenhagen-born bassist Jasper Høiby created the trio Phronesis in 2005, a group which gained international acclaim and toured extensively worldwide. Høiby continues to perform and record with a number of original artists while focusing on his own projects, the latest being Jasper Høiby's Planet B, an electroacoustic bass-led project whose debut release was included on *Bandcamp Daily*'s "The Best Jazz Albums of 2020" and *DownBeat*'s "Best Albums of 2020."

Titan #99: Hansford Rowe

Hansford Rowe, bass titan. Photo by Stevo Rock

Hansford Rowe is a fusion bass guitarist and a self-taught musician.

Titan #100: Angeline Saris

Angeline Saris, bass titan.
Photo by Subhrajit Bhatta

Angeline Saris has toured with the Narada Michael Walden Band, Ernest Ranglin, Zepparella, and currently fronts her own funk hip-hop fusion band ANGELEX. When not touring, she can be found teaching in the SF Bay Area and abroad at the Warwick Bass Camp in Germany. http://angelinesaris.com/

I really appreciate Angeline Saris, she is an amazing bass player.

—ANAIS NOIR

Titan #101: James Cook

James Cook's single "Grave Digger."

James Cook is a multi-instrumentalist/bassist/writer and producer based out of Nashville, Tennessee. His talents can be heard on many projects and stages with many of today's top artists. His skills in the studio as a bassist, vocalist, and engineer have been on countless songs and he has toured with Luke Bryan. https://jamescookbass.com/about

Titan #102: Jean Millington

Jean Millington—live and on stage.
Photo by Kenee Lee

They were extraordinary: they wrote everything. They were just colossal and wonderful, and nobody's ever mentioned them.

—David Bowie

Jean Millington, considered one of the best female bass players in the world, fronted the band Fanny and is known for her lyrical, danceable, and undeniably throbbing bass parts that propelled the band from the sixties through the mid-seventies. She also wrote and sang the band's biggest hit, "Butter Boy," and continued to play with sister June through many albums—*Ladies On The Stage*, 1977, to *Fanny Walked the Earth*, 2017—always thrilling her fans.

Titan #103: Kern Brantley

Kern Brantley played bass on Jimmy D. Scott's 2012 album, *Don't Stop The Music.*

A mere glance at Kern's credits reveal an individual whose talent and reputation for excellence earns numerous placements on major projects. Through his experience Kern has become a very accomplished musician, producer, songwriter and arranger. www.kernbrantleymusic.com

Titan #104: Kevin Keith

Kevin Keith and his Chapman Stick. Photo by Kevin Keith

Kevin Keith is a multi-instrumentalist, music producer, audio engineer, and Chapman Stick artist based in Los Angeles, California, and Reno, Nevada. Kevin's music appears on hundreds of national TV shows, webisodes, documentaries, games, and records. Kevin performs solo and with his band, the Electronic Jazz Ensemble. www.KevinKeith.com

Day 11: "Future Titan of Bass" Challenge Action Step

1. Visit http://www.bassguitarbeginner.com for Day 11 of the challenge.
2. Visit the "Titans of Bass" Facebook group (details in "How to Use This Book" section).
3. Visit the YouTube channel (details in "How to Use This Book" section).

Now we are going to shift to hearing the song without the bass track in place. You are going to supply all the bass notes. Ask your mom/dad/sister/brother/dog/cat if they have ten minutes in three days to watch you play bass on your very own song!

Play the song five times through without the bass track. Get used to this version, as it will be the song that you are playing live for your mini concert in three more days! Go for it! Practice playing along the song five times, or if you have more time, try ten times! Wow! You've come a long way. Practice the song all the way through at least five times in the "no bass version."

Tip: Download the new version "2: The Midnight Special—No Bass Track" from the titan website http://www.bassguitarbeginner.com/ and look for the link to today's lesson on the YouTube channel. Download to your iPhone/phone tablet.

Listen to the song without the bass track five times with your headphones every day; it should take about fifteen minutes total. This is an easy way for your mind to grasp what's happening so that you really get used to it being played without the bass parts. As you are listening, imagine you are playing the bass notes along with the song.

DAY 12
Cream of the Crop!

Simple, short, and sweet, the three Ss. This chapter is really a treat.

I asked my 131 participants this gem of a question and I was astounded to see (like most questions I asked) the diversity and also the similarity of the answers that I received. These answers are especially attractive because they contain both a mix of anecdotal stories and also a layer of what masters taught the masters. Also, they are seldom very intuitive—there is always a twist that I've noticed.

Here are some standouts. I feel it's better to let the artists speak out instead of me interpreting too much. This will be an ocean of the best tidbits and guidance from the best players in the world. Pretty amazing stuff really!

Let's Ask the Titans: What's the Best Advice Anyone Has Given You Regarding Learning the Bass?

The only advice I remember from a neighbor—I totally ignored. It was "Turn it down, you deaf *******."

—Mark Burgess

Get a teacher, practice, get better.

—Ron Carter

Connect.

—Armand Sabal-Lecco

Timing is the most important thing.

—Tom Griesgraber

You must never lose hope. You must believe in your dreams.

—Manou Gallo

Chuck Rainey once told me: "You need to be very serious about playing the bass, because it's the house where everyone else goes to find refuge. If you forget about being a bass player, you are leaving all the musicians and singers without a home."

—ABRAHAM LABORIEL

If in doubt, keep it simple and don't forget to listen to the space in between the notes . . . without one, the other does not exist.

—JUSTIN CHANCELLOR

They actually told me the wrong thing, and I kind of protested against it and went the other way. They said, "You can't play chords on a bass." I was already playing chords so I said, "Well, yes you can. I'm doing it right here." It was kind of reverse advice.

—BILLY SHEEHAN

Honeyboy Otis, the original drummer with Ray Charles told me: "As the bass player, think of yourself as the foundation of the building. If you move around too much, the whole building falls apart." When I worked with Elton John, I just followed his left hand for my bass parts—he didn't tell me what to play. If anyone wants you to play more, they will tell you.

—KENNY PASSARELLI

Years ago, Steve Smith, the drummer from Journey, and I were sitting listening to music. He said, "Listen to how the bass is fundamentally root oriented, and rhythmically supportive of the music." He says that's the way you should play. Early on when I was still very violin influenced when I played the electric bass, I was all over the place, and guys wouldn't want to play with me. He pointed out that the root is a nice note to play. Rhythmically, fundamental bass playing has great importance.

—JEFF BERLIN

The saxophone is a very organic instrument. A human has to play it and humans have to breathe. Sax players tend to phrase their lines in a very palatable and sympathetic way to most people's sense of music. It helps to learn the saxophone lines and transpose them to your basslines. If you practice these, you can learn to have tremendous phrasing in your bass playing.

—PHIL SOUSSAN

When I was young, my mom told me, "What does the world need, just another good musician? What the world really needs is good people." The point was that if we were going to spend all this effort, time, and attention playing music, it really needed to make us better people. The goal is to learn how to use music to make me better and the world better at the same time. A lot of musical education is about your sound and how to make you sound good. My instrument is not about my sound. It's about how I make the rest of the band sound.

When I was young and new to Nashville, I was doing a recording with trumpet player Wayne Jackson. He said, "Victor, you need to remember you have two ears. One of them is for you. The other one is for the rest of the band." That was his gentle way of letting me know that I could have been a better listener. He told me that I was a good player but if I learned to listen, I would be even better. I took that to heart and put it into action.

—Victor Wooten

Get yourself a good teacher. I studied with Bunny Brunel for many years. He forced me to learn music and get my technique together.

—Kyle Eastwood

I've gotten a lot from books and guitar magazines. One was a Kirk Hammett interview, where he gave his warm-up exercises, and he says he never starts playing until he does these chromatic finger runs, up and down the scale. That got me thinking that I should never pick up the bass without doing that. That became my lifelong warm up. It also helped me move all four fingers.

—Mark Stoermer

Record yourself. I started doing that early on with crazy contraption tape recorders and all kinds of wires when I played the records. As they say, "the tape doesn't lie." Playing yourself back and listening audibly is super valuable. These days they have Pro Tools [software] so it's way easier to record yourself.

—Jon Button

I remember a Tony Levin interview: "Don't worry about the negative aspects of being a musician. Eventually everybody gets replaced on a soundtrack during their career. There are going to be some disappointments with ups and downs." I also think that it's also good to not be overly influenced by the stuff that people say. I mean interviews like "do this or that" or that a "bass player should be this or that." Be yourself and play the way you think is right.

—Marc van Wageningen

Eddie Hazel, the guitarist from Funkadelic, told me, "You have got something. Don't let anyone ever tell you that you can't do this or can't achieve that. Follow your dreams to the fullest and see where it takes you. And I did.

—Shorty B

My career started when I moved to LA. I had a lot of good friends who were drummers. There is a camaraderie that is very unique between drummers and bassists. They told me, "Listen, it's great that you are stretching out and learning horn solos. But don't forget that you had better be able to lay it down and make sure the groove is covered." While I was expanding, I had to remember the foundation role that I had in music. That was very wise advice.

—John Patitucci

My college professor told me that bass defines the composition. Don't listen when people say that you are "just the bass player." You drive the bus, especially when you are improvising. Try to service the song as best you can without being boring.

—Julie Slick

I found out that having confidence in your playing is very important, no matter what level of player you are, from the very beginner upwards.

—Geezer Butler

Watch the drummer's foot. I pride myself in being able to play really well with a good drummer. If you have a good drummer, you can create the foundation—whether it's a live show or recording, it doesn't matter. No matter what the piece of music is, as long as there is bass and drums in there, that's the bedrock, the foundation, where everything starts from. So you need to consistently be conscious of what the drummer is doing

—Kasim Sulton

Listen to as much music as you can. Don't close yourself off to musical genres. There are a lot of guys who "don't like jazz" or jazz players who've never heard of Jack Bruce. If you want to be a well-rounded player, you need to get to a point where you really enjoy music and take music as part of your life and existence. I've learned this through listening and playing a lot of different gigs. This allows you to be a chameleon when you need to be.

—SCOTT AMBUSH

Learn how to read music. Learn as many tunes as you can. Learn the jazz standards. I was very fortunate when I was learning to play—a lot of the employment opportunities were in wedding bands, for older people. Most of the time they wanted to hear Frank Sinatra–type songs. Learning how to play the jazz standards will give you a greater understanding of tonality, of chord structure, harmony. They just have more going on than music that came after it.

—ROB STONER

To be a good, working bass player, you need to understand your role and embrace that role and love the role. I did learn how to play fast because I didn't want to bore people for a solo, but that's not why I love the bass. I love the bass because I love the groove. I like to be in control of the music's DNA.

—CHRISTIAN MCBRIDE

Listen carefully. Your job is to lock with the drums and be complementary. You don't have to play the same thing all the time. You can play different alternating parts, but it has to be the glue that holds the band together. We started out doing dances. You know pretty quickly if your rhythm is correct. If the rhythms are great, people just love to dance. You not only hear it but you can see it physically. I still get weekly fan mail sharing how the classic Blue Öyster Cult sound was amazing and not easily duplicated.

—JOE BOUCHARD

Get to know the "colors" of music. It's like having a painting box. Play overtop of the music until you get more experience with them. Then don't use all of the colors at once. Use them sparingly. Do your job and keep it simple. The rest of the band plays off of you and plays and interacts off your playing. You are all one piece of music. Pay attention to the length of your notes and where you place them. Learn the seven scales and modes and the seven chords. Practice with a metronome or a drum machine.

—WAYNE JONES

*In the 1970s there was a fusion drummer named Billy Cobham who was popular. I
was working sweeping floors at a music store. Billy was going to come through endorsing
TAMA drums. My boss had arranged that I would go and pick up Billy when he arrived.
I thought I was just going to pick up a guitar for delivery! I had twenty minutes with
Billy driving in my car. I told him, "I'm a young musician. I love what you do. How
do I do the same?" He told me, "If you want to make music your life, move to a place to
be immersed in music. Be around as many musicians as possible." This kind of sucked
because it was inconvenient at the time for me because of where I lived at the time. It
makes sense though. If you hang out with mechanics, you will get good at fixing cars. If
you hang out with the musician community, you will learn all about music. It was the
reason I moved to LA. It was 100 percent true.*

—Kevin Keith

*Be strong and build up the calluses on your hands. Be tough. It's the only way you're going
to be able to play. Mentally learn the music so you're coming from knowing the music and
not just coming from that one instrument.*

—Starr Cullars

*I remember having a conversation with Lemmy from Motörhead. I've been playing music
for literally my whole life. It's like I was almost born recording. I also came from a crazy life.*

*At times it got to me. I was mad about always being the center of other people's prob-
lems. It was starting to wear me out. I asked Lemmy, "Do you ever feel like it's too much?"*

*Lemmy knows I'm a vegetarian. So he says to me, "What would you rather be doing
for a living? Slicing bacon?"*

*I was like, "Oh man, y'know what? He's right!" If you are lucky enough to pay your
bills, do what you actually like and be creative every day, you are one of the lucky ones. I
wouldn't wish my life on my worst enemy but I wouldn't trade it for anything.*

*Learn to play the drums a bit. It will help you rhythmically when playing the bass.
It will also help you learn what the drummer wants from you.*

—Harley Flanagan

*When I was a kid we lived in Redlands, California, which is out in the desert. I used to
hitchhike to this community called Paris—not like Paris, France. I took lessons with this
guitarist Irving Ashby. He was in Oscar Peterson's and Nat King Cole's bands, a session*

guy in LA, and he retired out in Paris. He was the first one that really taught me to solidify my pocket. He would dance around the room and wiggle his hips—he called it the "funky butt." It was not funky from 1970, it was funky like hanging out with Duke Ellington and Ella Fitzgerald in Geneva. It was like the original funky. It made such an impression on me. I carry it to this day; I think about it all the time. He was the first person to tell me to leave spaces in my playing. As a young player, you think you have to fill up everything. He taught me phrasing.

—DAVEY FARAGHER

I realized I wanted to play bass after hearing "The Lemon Song" by Led Zeppelin. I was mimicking what I heard—I could pull it off by ear.

So I had a lot of great teachers—Michael Santiago—a guitar player in Jersey—great player and instructor, and he asked me to join his band. He's pretty key in my development.

—DAVE LARUE

Just play the groove and make it feel good. Years ago I was playing with some older guys in LA, when I was starting out as a fusion guy. I probably played way more notes then I needed to, funk and R&B tunes. The drummer turned to me and said, "Just play the groove, you don't have to play all those notes." He told me I was playing all this extra stuff that I didn't need to play, to just play the groove.

—DEREK FRANK

There is one piece of advice that my drummer friend, Ed Bernham, gave me when I was in a Motown cover band. What he noticed was: "Treat the bass like an adjunct to the snare drum." So the kick and snare goes 1, 2, 3, 4, kick, snare, kick, snare. When you hit the snare, whatever bass note you are playing on, stop it so that the snare is like the actual sound of an axe chopping off the note. I've asked people about that thirty years since—not one person has heard of that, or knows that that's a thing. Whether it's good or bad advice, how music works like that is always on my mind. I'm always looking for where the spaces occur, where they don't occur, how to make them occur.

—SCOTT THUNES

John McLaughlin told me, "If you want to play fast, you have to learn to feel it slow." If you are trying to increase the speed of a line, the idea is to have your metronome set very slow. For example, if your line is playing constant mid-tempo notes, you would have a relatively fast click, one for every eighth note. But if you internalize and are feeling faster notes, 32nd-note subdivisions, it's a way to stretch out the time spectrum, so you are anchoring it so your body can play fast and it doesn't stress you out like it would otherwise. I started to understand the relationship between my analytical mind and my intuitions. That was a game changer. I understood what the analytical mind does and what its correct function is. I think a musician can learn a lot by observing the basic function of the human mind and the body. When you understand something on a fundamental level, you progress very quickly. You can see that not everyone who has the same access to the same resources progresses the same. I think it has something to do with a combination of what you are naturally capable of and how well you grasp the spectrum of how you exist.

—KAI ECKHARDT

Someone told me, "Use your pinky. Keep trying and you will get it." And I'm sure glad that I did. It didn't occur to me to use all my fingers instead of three. Another piece of advice was, "If you switch those strings, it will be easier." I switched my strings from right- to left-handed playing—I used to play upside down

—DOUG PYNN

I've learned so many valuable things listening to other bass players, like Ron Carter. I got advice from other instruments who asked me to respect certain things. Drummers wanted a certain feel or view about what tight was. You have to get that right. Little things that were valuable were seeing other people using other kinds of musical statements and I could add to things to what I wanted to do. Miles Davis taught me the value of playing simple and the importance of the sixth interval. In his modal exploits, I learned about simple statements that were more melodic.

—HANSFORD ROWE

Tav Falco, who isn't even a bass man, told me, "Play a little bit behind." Larry, who's a drummer and producer, was looking at a song in Pro Tools, looking at the wave form, and said that the percussive guy, his notes only last a little bit, so if you play right on with him, you get some cancel out. So if you play right behind him, you play fatter, and there's no competition in the attacks. It's kind of hard to do, just a little behind—you'd be surprised how that works.

—MIKE WATT

I remember someone telling me, "Don't forget about root thirds and fifths." I worked out it was like a chord—first is the root, third is the chord. It started me off joining the dots, walking around chords. Obviously, not being taught, you have to work around it. You discover that if someone is playing an A, you don't have to always play an A, you can wander off, with these other notes. I started to then view the neck like patterns and shapes, not necessarily notes. I would see scales everywhere.

—BARRY ADAMSON

If you are going to take this seriously, you need to be comfortable playing anything in any genre. You don't want to be limited to being this kind of player or that kind of player. Whatever you do, make sure your jazz stuff is together, not just the bass parts. When you get more advanced, make sure you transcribe jazz saxophone solos. Listen to as many kinds of music as you possibly can. Make sure if someone calls you for work—whatever it is, you will be able to fill the bill. I know everyone has a specific genre they like. Be multifaceted. It helps with any type of music that you are playing. You take a guy like Marcus Miller, and he took Larry Graham to jazz, it's not like he is 100 percent a jazz guy or anything. He co-owns the first six Luther Vandross albums, where he didn't slap at all.

—BASIL FEARRINGTON

When I was really young, my junior high school jazz band was in the state big band competition. A director from another school said, "Hey, you really got a good feel—keep at it." At that strange age when you are just coming up, positive reinforcement is like gold.

—STUART HAMM

Some of the best advice I got is really advice that you get about music. I'm a musician who happens to play the bass. It's really about music and listening. One of the great stories that I like to tell is about Al Jackson, the drummer from Booker T and the MGs. We did a show together with the Jefferson Airplane at the Carousel Ballroom with Booker T and the MGs. I went up to these guys and said, "I gotta tell you, I love 'Green Onions.' I got it in the fifties when you put it out." There were very few hit instrumentals back in the day—a few like "Honky Tonk" with Bill Doggett, "Rumble" by Link Wray, and "Green Onions" by Booker T and the MGs, and Duane Eddy—but not a lot of hit instrumentals. In the late sixties, early seventies we played at the Carousel Ballroom, we did a show together. They were putting their stuff together; we were doing soundcheck. We were on stage. They were listening to our soundcheck. I went up to Duck Dunn and said, "You are the cat, you are really playing wonderfully"—of course, Steve Cropper and all the guys. All the work they did was fantastic, with Otis Redding, etcetera. Al Jackson said, "I've been listening to your soundcheck." Then he told me a story about himself.

He started out doing a lot of jazz before Booker T and the MGs. He was progressive on the downbeat. He had a short stroke on his stick like a jazz drummer does. He would come down slightly ahead of the beat all the time, giving it that lean-forward approach. He said, "Your guitar player is doing that. I listened to your playing and I like your playing. You are a unique player. In my opinion, you would help the sound of the band out if you just lean back on where you place those notes." He said, "Think of it as a seesaw. . . . one part of the band is on one end of the seesaw and you are on the other." He said, "You move back on the end of the seesaw and get that balance, that seesaw to even out to get balanced." The way he learned to do it was the short stroke he had on the snare. What he did was start his stroke up higher on the snare. By the time it came down to hitting that beat, on the 2 and 4, he had a longer stroke. He would hit it just a shade back of the beat. The rest of the guys were really more aggressive in the band, Booker T and Steve Cropper. It would pull the weight of the band back on their heels; it would give it some balance. It was the best advice that I got. I started thinking about that. It also gave me more time to fit what passages and notes, if I was trying to cram in everything I could. It would actually give room for the execution, so at the end of the passage, it would come out right on the money.

—Jack Casady

The best advice I ever got was from Marcus Miller. We were at a clinic in Toronto with him and I asked him about some techniques. He was talking about the idea of being a complete idea, like the technique was obviously important and you shouldn't pretend that you don't have to work on it, but you should be able to solo, you should be able to play solid basslines. An example was, "You would never ask a piano player if they knew how to play chords and take a solo. It's expected that a piano player knows the chords, to take a solo, to know the melody of the song, so bass players should expect the same for themselves." So that really stuck with me—I should be able to play the baddest grooves, take the best solo, and be able to play the melody of the song. And when you get that together, that's the type of bass player that I want to be.

—Jason Raso

Will Lee taught me how to play slap bass. He also taught me to put my pickguard back on to give me a place to rest my hand when I slap. So from then on I played with a pickguard on my bass.

—JEAN MILLINGTON

Funnily enough, when I first moved to London and turned pro and upgraded myself and tried to get in a big band, I used to go around to different people's houses, see if they wanted a bass player. I went to see John Mayall, Eric Clapton had left by then. He didn't say clear off "go away," but invited me in and played some tapes—that was a good thing. I found all these musicians had time for you if you were serious. John said, "Look, listen to what the bass is doing here. In blues, the bass is always landing on the one, the first note of the bar but, you can play around but it's always landing on the one. It keeps it more rooted, sort of a James Brown thing as well. I also went round to see Jeff Beck, who invited me in. He gave me a cup of tea, and said, "Look, if you can actually play the damn thing, you will always have a job. Learn your chops."

—BRUCE THOMAS

The first guy who taught me was a neighbor, Angus Thomas, who actually played with Miles Davis. When I left in 1985, he got the gig for a while. He was teaching me and made me play in a way that was solid and pay attention to those details early on, from the first lesson, get good sound, solid sound on the instrument, clean up my playing from the start. That was probably the most valuable lesson. Play the instrument cleanly. I think I get away with stuff because I play clean, clean up playing, not extra noises. That advice took me the furthest—being concise. Not strings ringing, manage how the instrument sings. One of my friends I played with a long time ago said I was a great musician but had a lot of maturing to do, so I started to play with less flash and covering the bases, being a bass player, using it in a way that facilitates the music.

—DARRYL JONES

Put the click on 2 and 4 when you practice.

—ANGELINE SARIS

This comes from Victor Wooten when I was at a camp: "When you are in a performance situation, try and play at about 70 percent of your ability." You want to go up there and do your thing. It relaxes you because you don't have to prove anything. When you have these situations, everyone is looking at you; he saw me tensing up. The other advice I think has really sat with me. I married my first teacher, so I'm still learning, getting private lessons. One thing he has implanted in me is the importance of being relaxed when you play. I would add relaxing in playing, sometimes we tense up and work against ourselves. Good technique can help the music flow through you.

—Ariane Cape

Early on when I was younger I was enamored by flash playing—that was what caught my attention. I spent most of my time practicing chops. I didn't have a teacher. When I started with an instructor, they took me to the foundations—what it was like to understand harmony and chords. I had the added benefit of getting my butt kicked in music. Learning as a young kid that it's flashy playing that gets you noticed, it's more about learning and focusing on reading, my tone, dynamics, overall groove, and pulse—really listening and having a well-balanced and well-rounded approach to my development.

—Adam Nitti

My bass mentor told me that I was not good. Every time he sees me playing, he says that I want to go back and practice, and he was right. It's important to take criticism—you can go and try to be better to prove to that person that you understand, that you listen. Put a lot of time in it, be dedicated to your craft. Don't play because you want to look good, to make money. Play because you feel like you need to get started, and you are good to go.

—Bakithi Kumalo

1. *Learn how to play the blues. The first song I learned how to play was a 12-bar blues song, riding on the root notes.*
2. *Lock in with the drummer.*
3. *My first teacher showed me proper fingering and technique; he was both a guitar and bass player. He showed me some great basic habits, proper consistent fingering. Your right hand is more important in terms of timing and dynamics.*

—Bjorn Englen

Make sure it grooves—that's why we are here. If we do our job right, the drummers, the keyboardists, and the guitarists of the world will feel free to do their job right. We provide foundation. That's where it begins and ends, regardless, of how complicated or simple the material will be.

—BRYAN BELLER

Holger Czukay (Can) reinforced in me the whole concept of "just play first and think about it later." This encouraged my style to play naturally. He told me, "Your playing is like Miles Davis, because as soon as you play, I know it's you. You must never forget that." That guidance reminds me of the old Yiddish proverb: "Praise nurtures the young. Criticism destroys them."

—JAH WOBBLE

Set up a goal of what you wanna achieve and then focus on your weak points in order to achieve that. Focusing on the weak areas of your playing will make the good parts sound way better as well.

—HENRIK LINDER

If you can dance, you can play the bass.

—HORACE PANTER

Play a lot and listen. Do what you want to do and keep doing it. You'll get good at it.

—CHUCK DUKOWSKI

"You don't know what you don't know." That is, it is important to search out teachers or someone more learned than yourself and always be looking for things to study.

—SHAUN MUNDAY

Bernard Edwards (from the band, Chic) sat me down and said, "Do whatever you want, mess about, go wherever you want, just make sure you are home for one."

—GUY PRATT

Think and play rhythmically—you're part of the rhythm section, so play something to help the groove.

—KINLEY WOLFE

Playing the bass is an accompanying instrument and it needs a completely different mindset from being, say, a guitar player. The bass player's job is to drive the music and inspire the solo players to greater heights. My guitar teacher was disappointed and told me I was throwing away my talent by taking up bass.

—LEO LYONS

Be open to all genres and styles. Then listen to it, and learn it.

—BLAISE SISON

Be yourself and never get comfortable with your current skill level.

—BUBBY LEWIS

Focus on becoming a better musician than you are a bass player. The latter will eventually complement the former.

—SHEM SCHROECK

Take risks! Fear of failure is the only thing that stops you.

—LIRAN DONIN

Think of the bass as a string drum.

—STEPHEN JAY

Use all your fingers. Press down hard on the fretboard so you don't get buzz. And feel it.

—SUZI QUATRO

A drummer at a gig told me to turn my amp down. I've noticed a lot of bass players play very loud either in their backline or monitoring. He pointed out to me that if I turned down, I could probably hear him and the guitarist better, and be better able to lock in and complement them both. Since then I've always turned down to the lowest level possible on stage. It really has improved my playing. It also gives the sound engineer out front a fighting chance of getting the band a good overall mix.

—CHRIS DALE

While in my first year of college, a guitarist dorm mate saw my bass leaning in the corner of my room. He said, "You play?" "Not really," I said. He told me, "Learn to play that bass, buddy, and you will never regret it or be out of a gig." He brought me over the first Santana record and the first Hendrix album and I was off.

—ROB RUIZ

Always play solid and big with confidence. Also choose the right bass for your hand and size, so that it's very comfortable to play.

—KERN BRANTLEY

A good rule of thumb for bass, and other instruments, is "if you can't sing it, don't play it." Don't try and noodle around just for the sake of noodling. Try to be able to sing along with what you do in your head when you play to try and come up with the parts. Also, when playing live, as an entertainer, make the hard stuff look easy, and make the easy stuff look hard.

—JD PINKUS

I've gleaned tons of advice reading interviews and watching videos. Victor Wooten's quite a good mentor—he breaks down difficult concepts about bass playing into very digestible, small bits of information.

—JAMES LOMENZO

I never strayed too far from the root notes. Showing what you can do is not conducive to being a good bass player. The other guys can show off but they need to know where "one" is.

—JIM PONS

I had a few hours with the legendary bass player Buster Williams in Harlem, New York. He was watching me very closely, I felt like X-rays. He made me feel that every note, every pause, every idea is 100 percent important in every moment. Nothing is casual, everything is deep, very deep.

—GINA SCHWARZ

To be patient and to start dealing with frustration, which is a feeling you will surely start to develop at a certain point of your path as a musician. You don't improve in one day but you have to keep studying hard every day to improve. Rome wasn't built in a day nor is any musician! So it's important to be patient: never give up!

—ANAIS NOIR

Someone said to me "silence is also music." I had the tendency to overplay in my younger years."

—MIKI SANTAMARIA

Learn your instrument as best you can, have fun while doing it, and play with as many musicians as you can. You are always going to learn something—it will never stop.

—Ronnie Dawg Robson

Keep the groove, hold down the groove!

—Oneida James

Be the right dress for every tune.

—Federico Malaman

Get into step with the drummer. Follow his bass drum. If you hit your note when he hits the drum, you move the song along.

—Gary Lachman

My dad would make me think about things and ask me questions. We would listen to a song and he would ask, "What do you think came first, the music or the lyrics? The bassline or the guitar?" Deconstructing a tune really inspired me to see if I could create something like that in my compositions. Those questions made me think about how the song was born. It's super interesting. This really made me think about composing and playing in the first place.

—Tony Saputo

Bruce Fairbairn, a famous producer, once told me, "Always try to play the lowest note— you're a bass player!" There are a lot of band members in straight-ahead rock bands that don't want you noodling all over the place. There's a right time and a place for you to solo.

One day me and Bruce were listening back to my bass track soloed separately from the rest of the instruments. When done, he turned toward me and said, "What did you think?"

I said, "I heard a few fret buzzes."

He replied, "That was the part I loved most about it. When I put it in the mix, it will add life to the track. I wouldn't change that for anything." That was a very valuable lesson that I've held on to ever since. Adding a human aspect to your recordings will bring them to life. Otherwise you can end up with a stale-sounding track.

—Scott Brown

I never really had any advice regarding playing the bass as I was really thrown into the deep end. Enjoy experimenting and try to become a good "all-rounder" in your style. This is so you can adapt to various musical adventures.

—Dave Pegg

Go slow. The best way to go fast is to start going slow. Never [rush] practicing anything that you can't play well on the instrument so you don't internalize bad habits. Don't feel like it's a race, take your time. Take those things you need to work on, focus and work on with intention. Take things you want to work on with the same focus with intention. Don't race through development. Take things step by step, give it its due time and attention. Build strong foundations to work on. Don't start with the hardest, most complicated lines. Simplify.

—Damian Erskine

My older brother told me, "Listen to and learn everything, even if you hate it. Don't be narrow-minded. You might learn to love that music one day when you are older. Even if you don't, you may need to understand it." If you are worth anything in the music world you may be called upon to play music that you thought you would never be asked to play. If you are into heavy metal, I think it's a good idea to listen to a Joni Mitchell or Barry Manilow record. Listen to what makes it great—the intonation, the timing, the orchestration, find the great in it, instead of saying it's not for me because it's too wimpy. When you are older, you might say, "I really love Return to Forever. It's a shame I didn't start playing it years ago." Most things that are successful are good. There is something great in it, even if it's not your bag.

—Daniel Miranda

I was at a bass player conference in NYC. I remember having a brief conversation with Anthony Jackson, the one and only time I met him. I said something about me having a light touch. I don't dig in on the strings. Naturally I play soft, but the note is big. I didn't need to hit hard to play. I felt insecure about that. Anthony Jackson said, "Other bass players have a light touch. It doesn't matter." It helped me own my identity as a player, like I was doing something right.

—Gail Ann Dorsey

In 1975 I remember Mick Jones from the Clash showing me the bassline from "I Want You Back" by the Jackson 5. It was amazing! Don't tell anyone, but he used to have long hair back then.

—Glen Matlock

I remember a discussion very early on in my career with Michael Brecker. He taught me to pay attention to the song and the drummer. I was never much for bass solos. I was into keeping groove and supporting and serving the song.

—Neil Jason

Boiling It Down

Bass-ically (sorry for the pun), here are some common themes from all the wealth of information.

BALANCE: Not playing too many notes, less is more, placing notes in the right places, don't overplay, leaving space between the notes, staying close to the root notes. Every note that you play matters!

RESEARCH: A healthy love and appreciation of many styles of music, listening and learning, studying many styles of music, being open-minded and curious.

PRACTICE PRACTICE PRACTICE: Consistent daily practice, routines, practicing the right things.

TAKE IT SERIOUSLY BUT ALSO HAVE FUN: It's a serious profession, but enjoying it is a smart move.

PLAY SLOWLY WELL BEFORE YOU LEARN TO PLAY FAST—GIVE THE DRUMMER SOME/KNOW YOUR ROLE: Remember that you and the drummer are partners that form the rhythm section—the foundation of the band. Lock in with the drummer. Your role is to make everyone in the band achieve peak performance.

DASH THE FLASH—LAY DOWN THE GROOVE: Fancy solos and flashy techniques are cool, but they shouldn't replace solid, groove-oriented basslines.

GET A GOOD TEACHER/MENTOR.

Introducing the Titans: #105–114

Titan #105: Rob Stoner

Rob Stoner, bass titan. Photo by Arnie Goodman

Manhattan native Rob Stoner graduated from New York City's Columbia College in 1969.

During the early 1970s, he became an in-demand session musician on many recordings, including "American Pie" by Don McLean. In 1975, Bob Dylan hired Rob as his bandleader and opening act for the Rolling Thunder Revue. He played and sang on several Dylan albums, including *Desire, Biograph, Hard Rain, Live at Budokan,* and *Live 1975,* while touring with Dylan. http://www.robstoner.com/bio.php

Titan #106: Jason Raso

Jason and his bass. Photo by Frank Nagy

Jason has been playing bass for the past two decades, with nine albums and countless live performances. https://www.jasonrasomusic.com/

Titan #107: Chris Dale

Chris Dale, bass guitarist formerly in bands including Atom Seed and Tank, now fronts his own band Sack Trick. He also hosts a weekly radio show. http://www.chrispaulo dale.co.uk/

Chris and his awesome outfit.
Photo by Visler Photo

Titan #108: Gina Schwarz

Gina and her double bass. Photo by Hans Klestorfer

Gina Schwarz is a jazz bassist/composer and winner of the "Music Maker Compositions Contest, Jazz 2002"; the Austrian "Hans Koller Preis" in 2007; and "Best Performances of the Year" in "All About Jazz—New York Best of 2007" in concert with "Bass Instinct." https://www.ginaschwarz.com/

Titan #109: Anais Noir

Anais Noir and her bass.
Photo by Coniglio Bianco PH

Anais Noir is an Italian-based singer, bass player, songwriter, and singing teacher.
https://madameanaisnoir.wixsite.com/website

Titan #110: Rob Ruiz

Rob Ruiz hails from the San Francisco Bay Area where he has played his 4- and 12-string basses with The Sorentinos, The Beer Scouts, and Rolls Rock. He has played onstage or opened shows for artists such as Van Halen, Jeff Beck, Captain Beefheart, Bob Dylan, Neal Schon, Dwight Yoakam, Bread, and Chris Issak.

Rob and his basses.
Photo by Aletha Ruiz

Titan #111: Federico Malaman

Federico, the bass dude! Photo by Dante Fiori

It seems to me an impossible thing to believe! Being part of this book is a great honor. It is a dream that comes true after years of studying the most beautiful instrument in the world: the electric bass!!! Thank you so much for this amazing gift! https://en.federico malaman.com/

—FEDERICO MALAMAN

Titan #112: Mick Harvey

Mick Harvey is renowned as a musician, record producer, and composer who has been active for the last forty-plus years and is perhaps best known as a member of The Birthday Party and The Bad Seeds and for his long-term collaborative work with PJ Harvey and Nick Cave.

Mick Harvey in black and white.
Photo by Katy Beale

Titan #113: Gary Lachman

Gary Lachman (aka Gary Valentine)—2003 solo album
Tomorrow Belongs To You.

Gary Lachman played bass for Blondie 1975–1977. In 1981 he was a guitarist on two North American tours with Iggy Pop. He was inducted into the Rock & Roll Hall of Fame in 2006. In 1996, Valentine, now Gary Lachman, became a full-time writer, with twenty-five books to his credit.

Titan #114: Armand Sabal-Lecco

Armand Sabal-Lecco is a Cameroonian bass guitarist, composer, and multi-instrumentalist best known for playing bass-guitar with Paul Simon in the eighties and nineties.

Be a voice, not an echo.
Photo by Paul Marchand

Day 12: "Future Titan of Bass" Challenge Action Step

1. Visit http://www.bassguitarbeginner.com for Day 12 of the challenge.
2. Visit the "Titans of Bass" Facebook group (details in "How to Use This Book" section).
3. Visit the YouTube channel (details in "How to Use This Book" section).

Practice the whole song. Listen to the song without bass notes in place.

Make sure you are ready to go for your mini concert in two days. Today, locate a recorder on your computer phone and record yourself practicing the song. Listen to the recording after you have played it through. Can you hear the bass in it? Does it sound even, or in time?

Is there anything that you can change? Can you play fewer notes, dragging them out more? Is the tempo in time? Be honest and record yourself three times after you listen to each version through.

This preparation will pay off for the concert. I'm so proud of you. You are quickly becoming a "Titan of Bass"!

Tip: Again, listen to the song "2: The Midnight Special—No Bass Track" without the bass track five times with your headphones every day. It should take about fifteen minutes total. This is an easy way for your mind to grasp what's happening so that you really get used to it being played without the bass parts. As you are listening, imagine you are playing the bass notes along with the song. As this version has drums, guitar, and vocals, it should be easier to follow along with the bass parts.

DAY 13
Reading Music

Do nonmusical influences show up when you play the bass? As we are getting close to the end, we can expand and learn about new things. This chapter delves more into theory and asks if it's necessary for a student to read music when they start playing.

I had a very close relationship with Miles Davis. He was kind to me in a way that people who knew him well were special. He was very supportive. He was very particular about what he wanted but at the same time he was always very open to experiment and wanted you to try new things.

People don't realize that he had an incredible sense of humor. My time with him was wonderful! Other than being born to my family, it's the best thing that could have happened to me. I am still learning lessons from my time with him. He told me to "learn how to draw and paint and cook." He said, "One art helps the other." I couldn't say it more simply than that.

—DARRYL JONES

In the early eighties, I did a tour with Stevie Nicks. She was into art, painting, and reading. She told me that she likes her songs to read like a novel and paint a picture for the listener. I started listening to her songs. Her songs are so visual that you can actually see the story hanging in the air. They are so classic. Now I try to see and seek out the vibe of the song. It's like the personality of a person to me.

—WYZARD

The thing is to not get too frustrated if improvement is slow. Remember music should be for enjoyment, not torture! At the age of seventy-two, I am now learning the cello. I can only do about twenty minutes a day where I feel I am progressing. The neighbors all have "For Sale " signs up on their properties.

—DAVE PEGG

Everything about your life determines what you play and how you play it. When you approach and play an instrument, it's just a transference of your emotions to the instrument. Your emotions come from the life you are living.

—Basil Fearrington

I urge all young bass players to learn how to read music and also play piano. Not so you can play it, but so you can play the chords on the piano and see how notes work in chords. Then you can put it on bass, which can help your playing a lot.

—Christian McBride

There are hundreds of years of musical traditions that should be taken seriously. Some incredible music has been created by means of it being transcribed. It allows us to take a glimpse into the past. It also allows much more information to be accessed right now for us to use. The writing of music itself is like an art form. It's like calligraphy. It allows you to easily communicate musical ideas with others. It allows you to create and retain music when you are away from the instrument. I've written a few songs when I was on the plane. All I needed was a paper, pencil, and eraser. When I was done with the flight, I had a complete song worked out. I didn't need an iPhone to do that. You are already a computer. You have all the software. You just need to access it.

—Kai Eckhardt

You shouldn't just rely on reading music. Music is a language that is passed on through hearts. No one is going to hear you read music. When we are babies, we first learn to speak before we write. Music is the same way. You should learn how to read and write. I do regret that I can't sight-read. I don't feel totally complete. The problem is people who read great can rely on it too much. So this makes their memory weak, even with great musicians. Some musicians would be astounded that I could remember seventy songs with whole forms. The more you work on it, the more you remember. Sometimes guys still look at charts after playing when they shouldn't have to.

You need to be able to read eventually. It amazes people how you can play like that and not read. It's because they have nothing to do with each other. When you look at Romani music, they don't know the individual notes. They just know how to speak the language with only their ears.

I was completely self-taught. It was good because it didn't give me any formalities. I can play anything that I want to. I do wish my parents forced me to read and write music. But as far as playing, I'm glad it happened that way. At some point, I was always going to go to music school, which meant that I couldn't take gigs for three years. I absorbed and observed a lot when playing gigs. It gave me a lot of chances to ask questions to well-rounded musicians that I looked up to.

—HADRIEN FERAUD

It is beneficial to learn the language of music, most likely mandatory if you want to be a professional (unless you're extremely gifted). I think learning tab is harder than learning to read music. You may as well learn the names of the notes, its time value, and how it's written down. If you learn music theory early on, you can envision what progressions sound like. You learn what chords and notes are most commonly used together. You can "see" progressions like 1-4-5, 1-6m 4-5 (like the CCR song "Lodi" and "Have You Ever Seen The Rain?") and other songs.

—STU COOK

You could be listening to music in every moment of every day. Everyone has a cell phone but I doubt they know the pitch, the key, the notes, and tempo of your cell phone ring. The biggest component to music is listening, more than knowledge. If we learn to listen to the world as music, how could you not get better at it? For many of us, music doesn't happen until you pick up the bass or listen to Spotify. For me, every sound produces a rhythm. For example, I can tell you that my turn signal in my Subaru normally ticks at 89 beats per minute. I know the pitches on my two microwaves—they are different. This makes me a better musician because my ears are constantly being trained. Listening drives music—it's where it all starts.

Bruce Lee is an inspiration to me and my playing. A famous quote of his is "learning martial arts is a study of oneself." Some people use martial arts to just beat you up really quickly. You can also learn to be so good that you could show the other person that there wouldn't be a fight because they messed with the wrong person. It's kind of the reverse—I want to play so well that I make those in the band show them how good they are.

—VICTOR WOOTEN

It might not be best to learn to read music right when you start. Some students might want to play in a band or play a recording so it could put the brakes on that if they had to read music before, so it's not a good prescription for that. You can learn musical theory without knowing how to read. You can learn pattern-based shapes, triads, etcetera. Some people who don't read music actually know more theory than they realize. It can be a difficult skill to learn on the bass, as it may be hard to read it. You could miss the beautiful shapes that have meaning. It helps them to use their ears more than other players.

—ARIANE CAP

Exclusive: Titan of Bass Starr Cullars and Prince: Part 2

If you remember part 1 of our story, Starr had a dilemma:

"You can come and stay with me while I finish and go out on the tour. Then I can get back to you and do your record." We talked some more and he ended up propositioning me three more times in the exact same way. I knew he had a reputation for the women, even young women like me.

I said, "Listen Prince . . .

—STARR CULLARS

Would she join Prince and wait for him to record after his album and tour? What Happened? On with the finale!

I said, "Listen Prince . . . I'm going to go back to school to finish. I'll be ready for when you finish that and then we can get together. So I left Prince and went back to school. I was working on my demos and playing with people in my hometown of Philadelphia.

P-Funk (Parliament-Funkadelic) came to town to play a show. One of my musician friends who knew them invited me to come with him backstage to meet them. So I took my demos and my bass, just like I did with Prince. I met George Clinton and the whole crew and gave them my demo tapes. I got called by them a week later when they were in New York City. I got invited to come up to New York, hang out with them, and then go to the DC show. I was hired by Parliament-Funkadelic during the time of the DC shows in 1992.

After I was hired, I told George my Prince story. George Clinton just happened to be signed to Paisley Park during this time. When I told him this, he said, "What? Well, you with Funkadelic now. We are going back to Paisley Park to do a TV show." Prince wanted all of his acts to do this whole TV show at Paisley Park. After I did my first European tour with P-Funk, we went back to the states and then went to Minneapolis. I thought, "I don't know if Prince is going to remember me." George says, "He's going to definitely remember you. C'mon girl." At Paisley Park, all the Parliament-Funkadelic group is there. Everyone is running after George because he is the king. George and Prince say "hi" to each other. Prince looks over George's shoulder and sees me standing behind him and says, "Starr? Starr Cullars? What are you doing here with George and the P-Funk?" Everybody is staring at me and thinking, "How in the heck do you know Prince?"

George is like, "Yeah, that's right, she's Funkadelic—you can't have her." We go over there, running over to George. Prince sends the New Power Generation to be my bodyguard. During this time, Prince and his management start coming after me to leave P-Funk and to come to him instead. So for my first two years touring with P-Funk, Prince would show up and try to get me to leave. It was a most interesting introduction to the professional industry. I had these two superstar legends using me like a chess pawn in their power games. It taught me a lot.

I stayed in the P-Funk and toured and I started opening up for them and Living Colour with my group. After that I only got to see Prince when he would show up at events, following me from a distance. I had to get older and leave to branch out on my own. By that time Prince was strung out and all the tragedy in his life that followed. I do regret not having the opportunity to work with him. I know that we would have written a couple songs and some cool things together. I am not regretful about the encounter with him. Most people have never had any kind of contact or relationship with him like this. I was thankful that we had had that connection, even though we didn't get to record directly. It was at the beginning of my career and I had his endorsement and his belief in me as a talent—way more than a lot of people got from him.

The only thing that I would be regretful about him was how he closed himself off in those later years. He didn't open himself up to myself or other people that could have saved him. When Dave Chappelle portrays Prince in his TV show, his impression was both hilarious and accurate. That's what makes it really funny.

Introducing the Titans: #115–122

Titan #115: Shem Schroeck

Shem wielding his bass. Photo by Izumi

Veteran of the stage and recording studio, Shem Schroeck has performed in all fifty states and in thirty-seven countries as a singer, multi-instrumentalist, and music director in a diverse range of genres. https://shemworks.com/

Titan #116: Bubby Lewis

Bubby has worked with Snoop Dogg, Dr. Dre, Lupe Fiasco, Jhene Aiko, Tha Game, and Kim Burrell. https://bubby lewis.com/

2019 Bubby Lewis solo album *Hero Dynasty*.

Titan #117: Blaise Sison

Blaise's blazin' bass. Photo by jamjimclark.com

Blaise is currently serving as musical director with The Family Stone. http://www.blazinbass.com/

Titan #118: Liran Donin

Liran and his double bass. Photo by Jonathan Trotman

Tel Aviv–born bass player, producer, and composer Liran Donin has been involved with high profile and cutting-edge artists. https://www.lirandonin.com/about

Titan #119: Joan Armatrading

Joan Armatrading is the first UK singer-songwriter and guitarist to gain international success.

A three-time Grammy Award nominee, Armatrading has also been nominated twice for BRIT Awards as Best Female Artist.

A recent Joan Armatrading album—
Not Too Far Away.

Titan #120: Manou Gallo

"Music and bass are my two life essentials."
Manou Gallo
Photo by Jurgien Rogers

Manou Gallo first performed at the age of twelve and went on to become a success, touring in various African countries and recording four albums. http://www.manou-gallo.com/

Titan #121: Kinley Wolfe

I like to play hard-rocking bass with a whammy bar and a touch of Memphis soul! http://www.kinleywolfe.com/; Instagram @kinleywolfe77

—KINLEY WOLFE

Kinley plays a mean bass. Photo by Jeff Stephens

Titan #122: Pete Trewavas

Peter Trewavas is best known as the bassist of Marillion and Transatlantic. He is also a multi-instrumentalist playing keyboards, guitar, and drums. He also is involved with engineering and writing music with Edison's Children. http://www.edisonschildren.com

Peter live in action.
Photo by Anne-Marie Forker

Day 13: "Future Titan of Bass" Challenge Action Step

1. Visit http://www.bassguitarbeginner.com for Day 13 of the challenge.
2. Visit the "Titans of Bass" Facebook group (details in "How to Use This Book" section).
3. Visit the YouTube channel (details in "How to Use This Book" section).

Listen to the recordings from yesterday and rerecord three to five new versions of the song. Try to get the timing in place and the tempo correctly. Remember, it's easier to play simply and make it sound good then to play too much out of time. For tomorrow: How are you going to play your song for your audience? Are you going to play YouTube on your phone? Can you play it on your TV?

For tomorrow, there is a special version of the song to play. Listen to it in today's lesson on the YouTube channel. Familiarize yourself with it so you know it tomorrow.

It's basically the same tune, but it has a little more time, about 30 seconds, before the song starts so you have time to get ready. It also gives you reminders on when it's about to start. It starts with a little intro and a countdown so you can shine. Start setting up your bass and amp in the area that you want your show. Move your bass and amp to the location and play it exactly the way that you plan to play it tomorrow. Play it three times through. Practice a "dress rehearsal" with a friend. Have someone you like or trust watch you play the song as you would play it tomorrow to see if the volume is good, and other feedback.

What to Remember for Tomorrow's "Performance"

What most people really notice when a band/musician plays a song is how the song starts and how the song ends. So practice these two parts and try to get them right. As long as you keep a steady tone and land on the right notes, you will be fine. Keep playing the notes all the way through. Remember all the times you listened and played along with the song. Remember, the drums are there for you to match; let your bass match up to the drum parts in the song. Relax, You got this!

♭AY 14
Ace of Bass

Words of Wisdom and Next Steps for You

Wow, what a journey! I'm proud of you! If you have made it this far and followed along every day, you should have a good taste of whether the bass is for you. You survived the bass challenge!

Today is the day of your live performance, so I won't overload you with information. There is some great advice at the beginning to help you with your first encounter of playing live.

Read the Daily Action step at the end to get some needed encouragement.

You stuck with it and it's awesome to see! As you have learned, there are always opportunities for bass players in our world. Is the bass for you? Are you a future Titan of Bass? Either way, thank you for sticking with the journey—I'm proud of you! I hope that I've inspired you to give the bass a chance. Who knows? Maybe you are going to try another instrument?

Here are some final thoughts and pearls of wisdom to help inspire you on your bass journey, with amazing advice for further avenues and areas to delve into.

Let's Ask the Titans: What's Your Advice for Playing Live?

Don't be overambitious. Start simply—that's what the idea of punk rock was. One gig is worth a hundred rehearsals by yourself. There is a bigger learning curve than playing a record at home for ten weeks. Don't be afraid to make mistakes in public. I was originally a harmonica player but was put on the bass because the bassist didn't show up. I had to play the bass live, even though I had never played it before. It was like baptism by fire. Suddenly I was the bass player. Life isn't always logical and thought out.

—Bruce Thomas

No matter how much you practice, one live gig is worth ten or more rehearsals. It helps concentrate your mind and get over stage fright and shyness. Just go for it!

—Glen Matlock

Learn it until you feel you are good enough. There is no substitute for doing live shows. When I began, we did all the clubs and played five sets a night. We would play for 45 minutes and then break for 15 minutes. Believe me that's how you learn your craft.

—Suzi Quatro

Playing live music is like boxing. Go and fight and beat the heck out of the opponent. I toured with the MC50 a few years back. I loved playing punk rock. It was cool to play the song "Starship" every night, as it's completely improvised. I had never done anything like that and I was fifty-four years old at the time. It was really fun and we played it differently every time.

—Billy Gould

Final Thoughts

Some young people think they have to be taught how to play bass. This attitude could be slowing you down a lot. You can see who is not waiting when you look at YouTube and see a four-year-old drummer killing it. In every case when you see that happening, it's because someone else in their house is killing it, too. Kids need exposure to music and opportunity, not formal lessons. First you display it, let them see it, and then give them an opportunity to try and play it. This happens with guidance and not overcorrection. Any beginner is going to make more mistakes and get it wrong often. The goal shouldn't be to have them "not be wrong" when they play and they are no longer trying to express themselves. It's sad because we could be fifty years old and still be afraid of messing up and making a mistake when we play. We learn to speak English when we are two or three. We don't correct babies when they say some words incorrectly. If we have freedom of expression—with guidance and no correction, then we learn to speak quickly. Lessons can slow you down if they happen too early.

—Victor Wooten

The mistake that I made when first learning the bass was learning bass riffs only. Instead of riffs, you should learn songs, vocabulary, so you can actually communicate with the bass. Don't just learn a riff with a "see you at the finish line of the song" attitude. It's better to be in the moment. You will develop your ear and rhythm at the same time. Ear and rhythm are really important to bass players. To me the politics of bass is: You look good making the other cats look good.

—Mike Watt

All over the world, in every single culture, we know people arrange music in tonalities of only seven tones or notes. They have never found a culture that divided the octaves in any other number. No one knows why this is so universal.

—Michael Manring

If you can learn to read notation, you can add a zero to your paycheck. And if you learn to sing, you can then add another zero to your paycheck. I don't get paid to play bass in the Steve Miller band—I get paid to sing. And I get to play bass too!

—Kenny Lee Lewis

Preparation is the key to auditions. The person that shows up prepared will more likely get the gig than the person that has more chops and isn't prepared. Preparation means learning the songs that the bands are playing. In my own audition for the Pink gig, I was up against a prominent bass player who had massively insane chops but she didn't know the songs. However, I knew the songs really well so I got hired. It was something as simple as that. If you take it seriously and do your homework, it shows that you care and will put the effort in.

—Eva Gardner

I have been able to work with a group of musicians that would go to college or businesses to show them the power of music. For the past few years we went to Stanford for the first week before school starts to address the new freshmen. We had a performance that would show them how music could help them plan out what their four years could be like. Music and being in a band is a great analogy for how we should live life. A band sounds better when all the instruments are different and sound different. In the same way, we recognize and celebrate our differences and be who we are. We all tune together before we play, so we all agree before we play. I don't know what to play until I listen to you. We would ask members in the audience if any of them have never played an instrument in their life. When people raise their hands we bring them on stage.

When I hand them a bass, they put it on and put their hands on the neck and strings—100 percent of the time they look just like a bass player. I don't tell them any of that. I then address the audience: "Look at this, I didn't tell the person to stand like this, don't they look like a bass player?" The very fact they act like this lets you know that this is not a beginner and it does them a disservice to treat like that. It's like the example of a ten year old who has really been listening to music for eleven years! They are not beginners to music, but only in expressing themselves with that instrument. I then look at where the left hand is on the string, usually it's on the fifth or sixth fret. I then whisper to the band what note the key of the song would be in based on that. I have the drummer start grooving. Every time, their head starts bobbing and moving.

I tell them what they are feeling in their neck and torso—that's music. We just have to put it in the bass. I tell them to squeeze their left hand on the string and let their right hand dance to the drums. Immediately, they start playing the bass! Then we come in around them and provide the rest of it. We start singing, "Everyday People" by Sly and The Family Stone. Larry Graham played a ton of groove with just that one note. All of a sudden this person is experiencing music from the inside for the first time. This is instead of being a listener who only experiences from the outside. All of these person's peers are out there watching as we are turning this person into a star. That's how good I want to be. To be able to take an absolute beginner to the instrument and we are still going to make you sound good. Then ask the audience: "If you were to walk in now and saw us playing, would you ever know this is the first time that he/she ever played any instrument?" We use this experiment to show how they can help each other in life and school. It also shows how you can bring a person up quickly because of how good you are. In many cases, we use how good we are to knock a person down instead. It's really a good demonstration to show the real power of music.

—Victor Wooten

Only a handful of bass players get paid to play a bunch of notes. The rest of us get paid to groove hard and make the band sound good. That's how I made my living. I've played on over forty albums in my career. I could pick and choose what gigs I wanted to. They trusted me to lay it down.

—Russell Jackson

The bass player is the unsung hero of the band. At one Uriah Heep gig, a technical difficulty caused the bass to drop out. It's amazing how many dirty looks I got with no bass. You can't have a band without the bass.

—DAVE RIMMER

Our role as sidemen is always the same. It's to do whatever the artist needs us to do.

They might want us to put our own stamp or to dictate how to play. We are there to keep the artists happy and make them sound good. I have that attitude on all gigs that I do. Different artists are different in their approaches and needs. But my function is the same—give them what they need.

—DEREK FRANK

As the bassist, you are the father that carries the entire family. The other instruments are like the kids that trust and follow you. This is why I was able to play with Paul Simon for over thirty years, because he trusts me. I consistently gave him what he needed on the bass. People who come to concerts don't care about bass solos, they care about dancing and having fun. Musicians who play to impress musicians can't get work. I'm sixty-four and I'm still working. I have experience, am consistent, and I know about this business. I really know how to listen.

—BAKITHI KUMALO

As a bassist you really are a team player. It's become second nature for me to always think about everybody else's parts instead of my part. I want them to be at their best. At the start of a series of shows, I'm so worked up about everyone else's parts and how they are going to do, how comfortable they are. I don't attend to the finer points of my material until the end of the tour. I don't mind keeping my stuff extremely simple. It doesn't bother me to not solo.

—JAH WOBBLE

It's a profession: be prepared, be on time, and do your best. Take it seriously. Some make the mistake of calling it "playing," but you are not out on the street playing baseball. This is a stone serious career and you should treat it and respect it as such. When you get called for a session and the downbeat is at 10:00 a.m., don't pull in the parking lot at 10:15. At 10:00, you should be in your chair, tuned, and ready to play. The artist may be an hour late, but that's their prerogative. You as the professional need to be there. It's an expensive proposition to make music, especially if you are in a traditional studio. Everybody's time is valuable, so it's really disrespectful when guys are showing up late and you are thinking, "I could have used that time for myself, but instead I'm sitting here ready to work, and you are waking up late and having breakfast."

It's like a practice, like a doctor or lawyer. If you want to be successful at it and have a career, that is. It's like when lawyers or doctors show up for work, they know what they are going to be doing. But as a studio musician when you show up, you have no idea what you are going to be doing, the kind of music or who the artist is. You get a call with a time, date, location, and you show up. You have to be prepared for anything that's thrown at you. There are certain professions where, if things don't go well, you can wait until tomorrow and give it another try. Call it a day. You can't do that with music. If you have one day in the studio with someone's project, you have to come in with a blank canvas and at the end of the day you have to leave with as close to a masterpiece as you can. There's a stress level that a lot of careers don't have.

—Leland Sklar

From a practical standpoint: If you want to play in a band and get calls from people, it would behoove you to learn from the groove masters. Learn how to sit in the pocket and groove all night.

—Christian McBride

When you embark on your career as a professional musician, you will have extreme ups and downs. It's the best feeling in the world when your band is first signed or you perform a sold-out show. This is contrasted with moments where you struggle. This is when you don't get called back after auditions, don't have gigs, or are faced with personality and drug/alcohol problems in bands. You need to think about the joy that you get from playing and keep going. Put faith in yourself and in your art. There are a lot of ups and downs. The downs can be brutal. Keep pushing, and at some point it will all seem worthwhile.

—Ben Ellis

I learned some important lessons in the beginning of my career as a musician. An internal part of the gig is showing up on time. If you show up one hour late, you are costing someone a lot of money. Make sure your bass and amp is working. Your job is to walk in and kick butt. It seems obvious, but not as obvious as you think. Leave your ego out of it and just play. It's amazing to see how much music can cause people to smile, dance, and buy records.

—NEIL JASON

David Bowie wrote a lot of his material by being inspired when listening to music. He wanted to re-create the same feeling while putting his spin on it. My favorite Bowie concert was at his fiftieth birthday concert in 1997. There were special guests like Lou Reed, Foo Fighters, and the Smashing Pumpkins and they were all at the top of their game. I was playing "Waiting for the Man" and I looked across the stage and saw Lou Reed and David Bowie. I thought, "Oh my god, how did I get here?"

—GAIL ANN DORSEY

Woodstock was a crazy good gig. The Woodstock film is still viewed by millions every year. CCR is included on the bonus DVD in the 40th Anniversary box set but was not included in the original film release.

—STU COOK

There is this great PC app called the amazing slow downer. You drop an MP3 into it and it slows it down. You can loop it and either keep or change the pitch. It helped when I was working on the song "One of Us Is the Killer" on the Dillinger Escape Plan on the Option Paralysis album.

I would get the drums and guitar track and clip out one section of it to slow it down to feel the groove. I would break it down into digestible chunks to slow down and learn it in a horizontal way.

—LIAM WILSON

Special Feature: What does playing football in the NFL have to do with playing the bass?

There can be a parallel between being a musician and being an athlete. In both areas you need disciplines like constraint practice, stamina, subtle nuances in performance, and good improvisation skills.

—CHRISTIAN MCBRIDE

Introducing the Titans: #123

Titan #123: Larry Lee

Larry Lee—NFL player and bassist.
Photo by Larry Lee

Larry Lee spent eighteen years in the NFL playing for Detroit, Miami, and Denver and served as vice president of Football Operations for Detroit. http://larryleeband.com/band.htm

I played bass in sixth grade. In high school I had to make a decision: either play football or play bass. I chose football. I put the bass down for twenty-five years.

After my NFL playing days, I was the vice president of the Detroit Lions. After nine years, that ended for me. Two years went by and I wasn't rehired anywhere. I then watched Pastor James from a Texas broadcast. He was preaching about reinventing yourself and following your passion. I decided to pick up my bass and get my fingers back in shape. I went around town and found some great Detroit musicians with some nice resumes. Here I am, eighteen years later with gigs all around the world. When I got out of football, I got my agent license. While I was taking the test, I saw Gene Upshaw from the NFL Players Association. He said: "Larry, you are a rare bird. There aren't a lot of former NFL players around. There are fewer former players that were high level executives like you. But you gotta be the only guy in the world that played in the Super Bowl, became an NFL executive, and then got to share a stage with both Chaka Khan and George Clinton!

I highly suggest that athletes learn a musical instrument. There is a natural coalition between sports and music. Being an athlete makes me try harder and be competitive. It teaches you to be part of a band, like a good team member. Learning music can help you learn rhythms to make you more of a fluid athlete. There is something about when an athlete becomes a musician, as they understand the role of practice and discipline in success. I've seen some musicians want to show up late, leave early, and make all the money. I don't agree. If you hire me to do something, I am going to do it to the best of my ability.

That's the athlete coming out in me. Preparation is the key. Like professional football, music is the survival of the fittest. To survive, you need to be good enough to stand out.

If you can make it in professional sports, it shows you have discipline. There is a certain level in the industry where you are doing shows and traveling. A lot of athletes understand getting up in the morning and staying up late, the 4:00 a.m. lobby calls. I was inspired by the life of the late Wayman Tisdale. His life opened up doors for me. He was a professional NBA basketball player and also a bassist.

I know how blessed I am. One memory that stands out was Super Bowl XLIII in 2009. The Steelers were world champions and we were the entertainment for the victory party.

Snoop Dogg joined us and we backed him on a song. It was amazing.

—LARRY LEE

Two major areas of success for playing in a band, according to Kenny Lee Lewis:

1. *When you want to play music with people in an ensemble, you have to use your ears and you have to play to the better of the good of the whole. You want to make sure that you are leaving spaces. Of course you have to support the foundation of the rhythm section from the bottom up. You have to leave space for other instruments to play. You have to get out of the way of that.*

2. *In general, to be around the band you have to respect everybody. Nobody is the star. Everybody is equal and part of the whole. Nobody is above anybody. Your ego has to get out of the way so you can be humble enough to become a good team player. This is the biggest thing that I tell my students who are trying to get into the music business professionally.*

Your playing and musical skills are about 40 percent of the success formula. Another 40 percent is your personality and getting along with people. The other 20 percent is a combination of hygiene and all kinds of stuff. It's a people industry—we are not machines and we are flesh and blood.

Playing is a small part of it. It's true that you have to be good at your instrument. Take care of that early in your life. It's great to "woodshed" and learn notation, structure, and theory.

But 60 percent of it is not music related. The stage is an intoxicating mistress and can overwhelm you. It will make you crazy if you let it.

—KENNY LEE LEWIS

Michael League (Snarky Puppy) and his band have a three-point test for hiring new musicians. The applicant has to:

1. Deliver the goods: They have to do all the things musically that they need to do. Have to have great rhythm, feeling, sound, taste, knowing when to play less or when to step forward, when to lay it out.
2. Be a good hang and citizen: They have to be someone that people want to be around on the tour bus/plane/hotel for the twenty-two other hours when they are not playing on stage.
3. Be dependable: Not being late all the time, but caring, solid, and even keeled.

You could be a wizard on your instrument but if people don't want to be around you, then it won't matter. You won't get the gigs or you will get fired a lot.

—JOHN PATITUCCI

Any band out there with hard, hard bass parts are the bands that are not making a lot of money. For the bands that are making the real money, like U2 or Beyoncé, the bass parts on the songs are more simple. When you are auditioning, they are really looking for someone who they can live with on the tour bus or plane. Everyone can play the gig, that's the easy part. Keeping a gig is way beyond what you are playing—it's who you are and how you relate to people.

—VICTOR WOOTEN

Introducing the Titans: #124–131

Titan #124: Tom Griesgraber

Tom and his Chapman Stick.
Photo by Bob By Request

Today Griesgraber is one of the world's most-respected and active performers on the Chapman Stick. http://www.thossounds.com/

Titan #125: Shaun Munday

Shaun Munday, bassist.
Photo by Starboard & Port

Shaun Munday captures audiences with soul-drenched vocals and show-stopping bass guitar virtuosity. https://shaunmunday.com/

Titan #126: Henrik Linder

Henrik's bass in a video. Photo by Dirty Loops

Henrik Linder is a Swedish musician and the bass player of the Stockholm-based band Dirty Loops.

Titan #127: Davey Rimmer

Davey Rimmer of Uriah Heep.
Photo by Richard Stow

Davey Rimmer joined Uriah Heep in 2013 on bass guitar and continues to provide the low end in the footsteps of Heep's classic rock bass players. http://www .uriah-heep.com/newa/biodaveyrimmer2.php

Titan #128: Shorty B

Shorty B and his bass. Photo by Michio Sacsha Key

Shorty B is a member of the Dangerous Crew and is a bassist and producer of 2Pac, Snoop Dogg, and Brandy.

Titan #129: Peter Griffin

Peter smiling with his bass. Photo by Michael Mesker

Grammy winning bassist Pete Griffin has played with top names in all music genres, from Steve Vai to Dr. John to Dethklok. http://petegriffinbass.com/

Titan #130: Russell Jackson

Russell Jackson is a superior, self-taught blues bassist who began his career touring with Otis Clay until BB King recognized his talent from the audience and offered him the position in his orchestra for the next seven years. From there he chose to pursue a degree from the Dick Grove School of Music, and then went on to play with such greats as Jimmy Witherspoon, Buddy Guy, Katie Webster, Bobby Bland, Charlie Musselwhite, Matt Murphy, Luther Tucker, Long John Baldry . . . and many more. "Find the pocket, play the groove, and you get the calls." www.russellbjackson.com

Russell Jackson, a BB king mainstay.
Photo by Jonella Jackson

Titan #131: Jeff "JD" Pinkus

JD getting ready to play with the Melvins. Photo by Patrick Houdek

JD is an American bassist best known for his work with American punk band Butthole Surfers. https://www.jdpinkus.com/

Day 14: "Future Titan of Bass" Challenge Action Step

1. Visit http://www.bassguitarbeginner.com for Day 14 of the challenge.
2. Visit the "Titans of Bass" Facebook group (details in "How to Use This Book" section).
3. Visit the YouTube channel (details in "How to Use This Book" section).

Wow! You made it: The day of your first live performance! You have come so far. Tips to remember for playing this show. Again, beforehand, ask a friend/family member for help to make sure that the volume of the song and the volume of your bass and amp are both set right. Because the song is only a few minutes long, it may go by fast. Make sure you try to enjoy it. The most important thing, or what people really remember when a band/musician plays a song, is HOW THE SONG STARTS and HOW THE SONG ENDS. Make sure you play solid consistent notes that match and lock in with the drums.

Bonus

Have a friend record the performance with a video camera/iPhone, and so forth. Post the results on the "Titans of Bass" blog, YouTube channel, and website http://www.bassguitarbeginner.com.

When you post your live performance we will send you a special Titans gift! Thanks for taking part in this challenge, you Future Titan of Bass!

Ɖᴀʏ 15
Bonus!

Congratulations! You've made it! Now it's up to you—Is the bass for you? Do you want to be a "Titan of Bass" like your bass hero? Please keep in touch on the FB group and YouTube channel to let us know how it goes and your future journey. As a special bonus, I have included some more songs to keep you going in your journey. I asked many of the Titans what song they played first. Many remembered what song it was, which is cool because some of the Titans have been playing for decades! Let's ask the Titans about what song they learned to play first to get some ideas. That also brings us to the next question, which is a little different. Rather than what they started playing with, what song would they now recommend that beginners start with?

Let's Ask the Titans: What Song Did You Learn to Play First?

A version of Mott the Hoople's version of Little Richard's, "You Keep A-Knockin'."

—HORACE PANTER

My first song was "Lucky Seven" by Chris Squire of YES, from his Fish Out Of Water *solo album.*

—SHEM SCHROECK

I played Chuck Berry's "Memphis Tennessee."

—PERCY JONES

"War Machine" by Kiss was the first song I learned most of.

—CHRIS DALE

The first song I learned was "Cheap Sunglasses" by ZZ Top—a really fun song. Rock and roll is a good place to start.

—ARIANE CAP

"Come As You Are" by Nirvana.

—Henrik Linder

I got asked to play the bass for a band audition at thirteen or fourteen. The guitarist asked me to put my finger on frets 7, 5, and 3 on a bass I didn't even own. I got the gig and never looked back.

—Liran Donin

I remember being thrown into a pit orchestra for a school musical theater production of Little Shop of Horrors *as maybe my first "serious" bass experience.*

—Tom Griesgraber

The first song I recall practicing a lot was "25 Or 6 To 4" by Chicago.

—Shaun Munday

The first song that I learned was "Knock On Wood." The band I played with didn't have a bass player so I had to play it. You could play it with two open strings with two changes. It got me fired up very quickly. Suddenly that's all I was interested in. I put in the hours and the rest is history.

—Neil Jason

For me it was "Smoke on the Water" by Deep Purple. It's one of those easy basslines that has everything. If you get the essence of that song, you will learn about groove and tone.

—Brad Smith

Wow, great stories. A lot of good info here. Here are some other great choices to learn on your journey.

Let's Ask the Titans: What Song Should an Absolute Beginner Start With?

I would suggest a bass player learn how to play "I'm Eighteen" by Alice Cooper. It's a simple song in E minor and Dennis' bass part is genius and classic. I recently did a lecture for high school. We played Led Zeppelin's "Rock And Roll." I was able to get the whole class—bass, drummer—and showed them what to play. We dived right into it quickly and had a great time. "Louie, Louie" is a little more sophisticated than you might think, yet it's just three notes. The chorus has one feel, then the verse has another, different feel. You have to time them just right. I've taught this to many kids over the years. It's simple and a good place to start.

—JOE BOUCHARD

"Dazed and Confused" by Led Zeppelin. Don't listen to the tab unless you absolutely have to. I am so anti-tab. It's a fun song and challenging. It will also teach you patterns that apply to all the strings.

—TONINA SAPUTO

"With Or Without You" by U2. "Manic Depression" by Jimi Hendrix. Both gives you a chance to try to play on the record and work on rhythm and timing and to move some fingers on the fretboard.

—MARK STOERMER

"With Or Without You" by U2. It's just four notes (D, A, B, and G) and it never changes.

—MIKI SANTAMARIA

Start with Booker T and the MGs' "Green Onions." It's pretty simple and it swings. The pattern stays the same through all the chord changes. It has a good feel, and it's fun to play. Booker and the MGs were close friends with CCR. I stayed at Duck Dunn's house in Memphis a few times.

—STU COOK

Fortunately, I had the sense to know that if you couldn't play in time, then it wouldn't matter what you played. When I started, James Jamerson and Paul McCartney were doing lines that were way over my head. The first riff I learned was "Green Onions." It had three notes. I also learned to play "Wipeout" by the Ventures and "You Really Got Me" by the Kinks. These are good places to start.

—BRUCE THOMAS

"Stars in Your Eyes" by the Dramatics.

—BUBBY LEWIS

The riff for "Iron Man" is a good one to start with. It is fairly simple and straightforward.

—GEEZER BUTLER

Find something that you've been listening to for a while, preferably something with a bass part that's simple and repetitive. When I was learning, it was riff rock like Cream's "Sunshine of Your Love."

—JAMES LoMENZO

"Another One Bites the Dust" by Queen. John Deacon is so underrated. He's as good as Entwistle and all the other bass heroes.

—GAIL ANN DORSEY

"Everyday People" (Sly and The Family Stone) and "Everyday I Have The Blues" (BB King).

—BLAISE SISON

Learn "Satisfaction" or "Sunshine of Your Love." Both have two of the most memorable opening riffs. If you can learn those, you're on your way.

—GARY LACHMAN

"Africa" by the Meters. It has a simple bass line with the phattest groove ever.

—GEORGE PORTER JR.

The first song a beginner should learn is something with a fairly simple, repetitive bassline like:

> *"The Big Payback" by James Brown*
> *"Uptown Funk" by Mark Ronson ft. Bruno Mars*
> *The "A" section of "Chameleon" by Herbie Hancock*
> *"Xxplosive" by Dr. Dre or "25 Or 6 To 4" by Chicago*

—SHAUN MUNDAY

"Psycho Killer," Talking Heads. If ever there was a bassline that served the song—this is it.

—MARK BEDFORD

"A Forest" by The Cure has a simple but totally satisfying bassline—melodic, repetitive, and rhythmic—with small subtleties that encompass just enough notes to get you going.

—JUSTIN CHANCELLOR

I think for a beginner a song like "Peter Gunn" by Henry Mancini and also "The Blues Brothers" theme song. It's a riff that sounds familiar and it gets all your fingers working.

—KINLEY WOLFE

Any basic rock and roll tune where the bass part is the standard line. Chuck Berry or Little Richard songs are good.

—SUZI QUATRO

"You Really Got Me" by the Kinks.

—EVA GARDNER

Pick something you absolutely love. The first song that I learned was the Adverts single called "Quickstep." From there I learned every song on Crossing The Red Sea With The Adverts *and "Rattus Norvegicus" by The Stranglers.*

—MARK BURGESS

"Seven Nation Army" by the White Stripes
"Free Fallin'" by Tom Petty
"Knockin On Heaven's Door" by Bob Dylan
"When I Come Around" by Green Day
"Sunshine of Your Love" by Cream
"It's Your Thing" by the Isley Brothers
Jazz standards like "Song for My Father," "Autumn Leaves" and "Girl from Ipanema"

—ONEIDA JAMES

"Seven Nation Army" by the White Stripes.

—ROB RUIZ

I'd go with either "Wild Thing" by the Troggs or "Louie, Louie" by the Kingsmen, in A! It's pretty much three notes. It's so primal. You can even play the open strings to make it easier! Rock out!

—MARY HUFF

"Rain" by the Beatles, "You Really Got Me" by the Kinks, "Louie, Louie" by the Kingsmen.

—STEPHEN JAY

"Louie, Louie."

—JIM PONS

We want to hear from you on your progress! That's why we want to hear about your journey and progress in our Titans of Bass Facebook group https://www.face book.com/groups/2548463212118457; website http://www.bassguitarbeginner .com and YouTube channel https://www.youtube.com/channel/UCPTsxR-dP0 _zGgKVaJ6SFpg. Please post songs you are learning, songs that you want to play, and so forth. Thanks for taking the challenge and finding out if the bass is for you!

—KJ Jensen

Index